Teaching Dance Improvisation

Teaching Dance Improvisation serves as an introduction to, and a springboard for the author's theories, practices, and curriculum building of dance improvisation as a technique. By taking a similar approach to teaching ballet, modern, jazz, tap, or hip hop, this book supplies its reader with an easy-to-follow roadmap in order to begin building and incorporating dance improvisation into dance studios/classrooms and curriculums.

Matthew Farmer is Chair of the Dance Department at Hope College and the Dorothy Wiley DeLong Endowed Professor of Dance. He is the former Co-Artistic Director of R.G. Dance Productions, current Co-Artistic Director of H2 Dance Co., and co-author of the book *Introductory Modern Dance: A Teaching Manual*. Matthew received his MFA from the University of Michigan in Dance Performance and Choreography, and his BA in Theatre and Dance from Hope College. Matthew was a company member of The Peter Sparling Dance Co., company member and Associate Director of LehrerDance, and has performed as a solo artist in the United States, Germany, Belgium, and the United Kingdom. Farmer's choreography has been produced by college and university dance programs, professional dance companies, international festivals, theater companies, dance competitions, and musical theater venues throughout the United States, Germany, the United Kingdom, Mexico, France, and Ecuador. As an educator, Matthew focuses on modern dance, contemporary dance, jazz dance, improvisation, partnering, and dance composition.

Routledge Advances in Theatre & Performance Studies

This series is our home for cutting-edge, upper-level scholarly studies and edited collections. Considering theatre and performance alongside topics such as religion, politics, gender, race, ecology, and the avant-garde, titles are characterized by dynamic interventions into established subjects and innovative studies on emerging topics.

Applied Theatre and the Sustainable Development Goals
Crises, Collaboration and Beyond
Taiwo Afolabi, Abdul Karim Hakib, Bobby Smith

Dancing Shakespeare
Ballet Adaptations of William Shakespeare's Works from the Eighteenth Century to the Present
Iris Julia Bührle

Teaching Dance Improvisation
A Beginner's Guide
Matthew Farmer

1000 Ways to Ask Why
Introduction to Dramaturgical Thinking
Emily LeQuesne

Making a Scene
Creating a Scene Study Class for Actors
Bill Gelber

For more information about this series, please visit: www.routledge.com/Routledge-Advances-in-Theatre--Performance-Studies/book-series/RATPS

Teaching Dance Improvisation

A Beginner's Guide

Matthew Farmer

Routledge
Taylor & Francis Group
LONDON AND NEW YORK

Designed cover image: Paul Willard

First published 2025
by Routledge
4 Park Square, Milton Park, Abingdon, Oxon OX14 4RN

and by Routledge
605 Third Avenue, New York, NY 10158

Routledge is an imprint of the Taylor & Francis Group, an informa business

© 2025 Matthew Farmer

The right of Matthew Farmer to be identified as author of this work has been asserted in accordance with sections 77 and 78 of the Copyright, Designs and Patents Act 1988.

All rights reserved. No part of this book may be reprinted or reproduced or utilised in any form or by any electronic, mechanical, or other means, now known or hereafter invented, including photocopying and recording, or in any information storage or retrieval system, without permission in writing from the publishers.

Trademark notice: Product or corporate names may be trademarks or registered trademarks and are used only for identification and explanation without intent to infringe.

British Library Cataloguing-in-Publication Data
A catalogue record for this book is available from the British Library

ISBN: 9781032479989 (hbk)
ISBN: 9781032480381 (pbk)
ISBN: 9781003387084 (ebk)

DOI: 10.4324/9781003387084

Typeset in Optima
by codeMantra

Contents

	Acknowledgments	vii
	Introduction	1
1	What Is Improvisation?	6
2	The 10 Rules of Improvisation; Plus 1	17
3	Rule #1 – There Is No Right or Wrong… But Sometimes There Is a Better Choice	35
4	Rule #2 – Follow Your Impulse	47
5	Rule #3 – Start with What You Know	59
6	Rule #4 – When in Doubt, Go Back to the Beginning	71
7	Rule #5 – The Moment You Check Out, Someone Gets Hurt	84
8	Rule #6 – It Takes a Village to Raise an Improvisation	100
9	Rule #7 – The Hardest Part Isn't Knowing When to Start: It's Knowing How to Start	112
10	Rule #8 – Everything You Need Exists in the World around You	127

11	**Rule #9 – Continual Movement in and of Itself Is Not Necessarily Improvisation**	143
12	**Rule #10 – Be Wary of the Black Hole**	156
13	**Plus 1 – Repetition Is Comfort Food**	163
14	**Additional Considerations and Concluding Thoughts**	172
15	**Sample Class Curriculums**	179
	Index	189

Acknowledgments

Before we begin our journey together in the coming pages, I want to take a brief moment to recognize and thank the various individuals and groups who have both made this book and my longtime career a possibility. I have always believed that it is best practice to give credit where credit is due, and to remind myself daily that I am (in my opinion) one lucky individual.

First, I must pay reverence to the many teachers, instructors, choreographers, and mentors who spent hours and years of their lives pouring into me. My journey into the dance world did not begin until college, and it was my first improvisation class that sparked both my love and passion for both dance and improvisation. Because of these many individuals and their never-ending patience with me, I was able to enter the professional world of dance and live a life that a young boy born in the middle of farm country could have only imagined. Thank you to these individuals. You know who you are, and I am forever indebted to you.

Second, I need to thank my family. My wife (in particular), daughters, brother and sister, parents, and those close friends whom I consider family have all seen the best and the worst of me. Despite the many ups and downs, they have remained my rock and compass pointing north. All my love to each of you and thank you for always believing in me.

Third, it is only fitting that I specifically thank the many improvisation teachers and practitioners who not only showed me the way of dance improvisation but encouraged my younger self to dive deeper, experience more, and to simply keep trying. They welcomed me into their communities with open arms, and for that, I am forever grateful. While this book contains my own ideas and philosophies on teaching beginning dance improvisation, it is a culmination of the many theories and concepts taught to me by my mentors. Their ways are

Acknowledgments

my ways, and I hope this book positively adds to an extensive filed of books, articles, and classes addressing dance improvisation.

Finally, I write this book as a love letter (of sorts) to dance studio teachers, owners, and public-school dance instructors. You are not only teachers, but you are also surrogate parents, mentors, and friends for the many young dancers who enter your spaces. I count myself lucky to know many of you, and as you read the following pages, please know that this book was written out of earnest admiration for each of you. Your time is limited and your resources small, but despite these ever-present pressures, you still manage to teach, motivate, and transform the next generation of dancers. Many of you have asked for a book such as this. May this guidebook be a supportive and enjoyable resource as you continue to do the much-needed work of teaching and inspiring the dancers, movers, and artists of the next generation.

Introduction

It's inevitable. Every time I enter the studio or convention center to teach an improvisation class, I lock eyes with someone in the room, and in that moment, I witness one of three reactions. All three of these reactions are real and visceral, and each breaks my heart. The first reaction is the student who stares at me wide-eyed, fear gripping their body, because they have (at some point) experienced an improvisation class where they were taken so far out of their comfort zone that they made the promise to "never do this again." The second reaction is the student who stares down all others in the class, plotting the best tricks they will execute in hopes of being "the last dancer standing." The final reaction usually comes from a teacher. I can see that they love improvisation, and are excited for their students to try it, but are fearful that this will be another class in a long list of classes where their students are either left unfulfilled or with an impression that improvisation is only about product.

Context

It has been my long desire to codify a way of teaching dance improvisation in a manner that remains true to its creative and intellectual nature, while simultaneously making it accessible and enjoyable for beginners. Too often, I have found that dance improvisation has been taught from one of two extremes: intellectual or accessible. Because of this, dance improvisation has often been relegated to mere tasks and games meant for the production of choreography, as a means of showing physical prowess, or an intellectual endeavor with no real accessible entry point. While none of these are wrong in and of themselves, they inherently sacrifice the others in pursuit of a singular focus. This book seeks to change that trend.

The 10 Rules of Improvisation: Plus 1 is my own personal and developed pedagogical approach to teaching dance improvisation to beginners, and those

Introduction

who have turned away from dance improvisation due to a previously undesirable experience. These guidelines are also for those teachers who love improvisation but may struggle with how to incorporate what they learned in their own personal training into a classroom or studio setting. Lastly, this pedagogical approach is for any dance teacher who may be asking themselves, "Why should I care about dance improvisation?" All three of these situations have individual and justifiable reasons for being wary of dance improvisation, and yet, I would argue they all stem from the same place: teaching and experiencing dance improvisation can feel very inaccessible at times. Let's be honest, it many times doesn't make curricular and business sense when propped up against the other dance forms we teach.

Because of this frustration, I have seen dance improvisation as an add-on to other dance forms or composition class; rather than a technique in and of itself. It has been used as a tool in service to choreography, rather than a thing of stand-alone value. This outcome is understandable since teaching dance improvisation can, at times, feel like trying to nail Jell-O to a wall; the moment you think you have it, it all slips away. Additionally, its inherent nature (imagination and self-expression) can make it difficult to build a progression-based curriculum. Therefore, it may at times simply be easier to put improvisation on the shelf as a resource, rather than build a curriculum that places it in the realm of, shall we say, "dance technique."

This tug-of-war, the tension between clear progressive curriculum and free-based exploration, is why I developed these rules and why I have written this book. While these rules (or perhaps think of them as guidelines) are not the only method for introducing and teaching dance improvisation, they are clear and concise starting points for any interested instructor to begin. Too often, I have witnessed students and teachers leave dance improvisation due to frustration, exhaustion, and/or a sense that it is only for play. This is why my heart breaks: generations of teachers and dancers have missed the creative, artistic, and, yes, physical benefits provided through an accessible dance improvisation curriculum. In essence, we have been robbed of a world that offers so much simply because the pathway was unclear.

Perhaps this whole notion is best summed up through the promise I make to students in every beginning improvisation class I teach. I promise the students that I will not (to reference an earlier story) make them "be a tree," and I will do my best to gently take them out of their comfort zones. In return, I ask them to make me a promise. If I uphold my end of the bargain they must, in turn, promise to take risks, support one another, and ultimately be willing to laugh at both me and themselves. In making this pact we as a collective set a foundation for the practice and participation of the class. I now make you a similar promise. I will do my best to remove the mystery that sometimes surrounds dance improvisation and provide you with clear progression-based theories and exercises as a starting place from which you can build your own curriculum. In turn, I ask that you participate fully in this book. Please write in the margins, highlight insights you discover, disagree with me, seek out additional sources that can add to what you will learn, or contact me so that together we might continue this learning in real time.

Considerations

With this contract now established, let us establish a few ground rules before we begin.

1. This is, in fact, an introductory book. No singular book can ever fully unpack and teach the years of experience of its author and the decades of wisdom handed down by the foundational practitioners and creators of improvisation. After all, I would argue that dance improvisation has been a part of dance since the beginning of time.

    If we look at cultures across the globe, we can see its existence in social dances, dances of worship, and, believe it or not, dance training: both past and present. It is only since the early 1970s that dance training in the United States (more specifically, certain dance training) has tried to codify ideas and meaning behind improvisation. Therefore, I highly recommend finding a mentor with whom you can ask questions and gain clarification. This book is meant to serve as a beginning resource to start you on your journey. However, finding a trusted and knowledgeable practitioner who can guide you through your questions, challenges, and successes is always best practice. Guest instructors, consultants, master classes, and workshops (both for your teachers and your students) are great ways to begin this introduction to dance improvisation, as well as the continued experience and practice of it.

2. This book is meant to guide you toward the beginning of your curricular development for your students and/or studio. You and you alone know your students, your community, and the external factors affecting your business better than anyone else. As a studio owner or teacher, you have spent a

lifetime cultivating relationships with parents and their children as well as community leaders, local organizations, your school, and other arts organizations in your area, and therefore, you know best the entry point, pace, and ultimate endgame that is most fitting for your dance improvisation curriculum.

Therefore, do not be bogged down if you have to adapt exercises in this book, or, perhaps, need to throw them out entirely. Again, best pedagogical practice says "walk into the room with a plan (ideally more than you need), and adapt that plan according to the bodies in front of you." May this book be a springboard and/or foundation on which you will eventually build your own dance improvisation curriculum.

3. Additional influences outside of the dance field are strewn throughout this book. The purpose behind this is twofold: (a) to allow us to see that all things in life are connected, and (b) to make this book (like the pedagogy it promotes) accessible. The more we can begin to see the interconnectedness between life and what we teach in the studio/classroom, the more our own learning and educational growth will exponentially expand. Similarly, the more we can learn to enjoy and laugh at our learning process, the easier it becomes to feel comfortable, let go of preconceived notions, and, ultimately, take risks.

4. Have "Serious Fun." I use this specific phrase because I feel much of dance improvisation's history is full of situations that encompassed only one part of this statement. Historically, I have seen situations where students have either "Had Serious," creating an environment where no creativity can occur because it was so stressful and philosophical that they were too afraid, or too lost, to make a decision, or they "Had Fun," creating a free-for-all environment that ended with either a student being injured, or left parents wondering why they were paying for this class. Therefore, it is the combination of the two (seriousness and fun) that guide this book's pedagogical approach.

5. Always remember joy. Ultimately, improvisation, at its core, is about personal creativity, exploration, and self-expression. While there are deep and thought-provoking discoveries to be made, we must never forget that joy-filled innovation is the basis for dance improvisation.

6. I encourage you to NOT read this book from cover to cover in one sitting. Rather, might I suggest reading one chapter at a time, pausing in order to consider the ideas and exercises discussed. This process will allow for you

to also think about possible additional exercises you have either learned in your past, or perhaps new ideas and exercises spurred on by the information supplied in the chapter you just read. In either case, please treat this book as a workbook, rather than something sacred.

7. Remember, these rules are my principles. They are by no means the only way to teach dance improvisation, but they are the manner by which I have found the most success in introducing dance improvisation in a manner that excites both students and teachers. If it is helpful, perhaps change the word "rules" to the word "guidelines" throughout your reading.

8. You will begin to pick up a pattern as you read this book. Each chapter begins with both the theories behind that chapter's rule, as well as historic and cultural context on how and why I developed each rule. Each chapter ends with a series of exercises meant to highlight the chapter's lesson, as well as prepare you for the next chapter. While I personally would not recommend skipping the first half of each chapter, if you are in a pinch and need a quick reference to exercises, feel free to jump right to the end of each chapter.

Try

Now, with these ground rules and hints in place, let us prepare to take flight into my 10 Rules of Improvisation: Plus 1.

What Is Improvisation?

Introduction

Before we dive into curriculum and theory, let us first begin with the concept of what dance improvisation is. This again can be a fairly lengthy discussion that could (in theory) last this entire book. To avoid spending an unforeseen number of pages debating and counter arguing what dance improvisation is, let me first begin with some advice from my father; "Son, ninety percent of life is knowing what you don't want to do."[1] I find this guidance extremely helpful when discussing dance improvisation. Rather than try to quantify every nuance that exists within dance improvisation (after all, I might as well try to quantify love while I'm at it), let me briefly discuss what I have dance improvisation not to be.

Context

Dance Improvisation Is Not Doing Whatever We Want, Whenever We Want

I'll never forget an experience I had early in my dance training. I was taking the second improvisation class of my early career as a dancer and was loving every minute of it. However, toward the end of the semester, I began to notice that the class became repetitive and predictable. Particularly, I began to ask myself, "Is this all there is?" In each class, all of the students eventually worked themselves into a frenzied, hour-long improvisation, where none of us noticed, or perhaps even cared, what any other student was doing. We were, quite literally, living in our own small, creative worlds. This was the beginning of my journey toward exploring dance improvisation as a cooperate experience; one that still possessed the same joy and freedom of individual creative practice but served a larger purpose than my own desires and gratification.

I understand my comments could sound completely counterintuitive to the idea of dance improvisation but hear me out. Yes, dance improvisation is about personal movement exploration and spontaneous creativity. At its core, it is about the joy and freedom one can experience by using and expanding their movement vocabulary (or what I like to call the **Human Movement Buffet**). However, dance improvisation merely as a means of self-serving ecstasy can easily lead to a destination where there is little room for others. In other words, the practice of improvisation for mere personal movement advancement can negate the joy of communal practice and shared corporate experience. A simple example of this idea would be improvisation within a breakdancing cipher (i.e. dance battle). While the individuals competing inside the cipher are most certainly focused on their own movement generation, they are simultaneously focused on the movement laid before them by their competitors, as well as the overall reaction of the crowd surrounding them. This shared experience of give-and-take can many times lead to even more creative choices: ones that would never have been discovered if it were left to individual exploration.

A final note on this topic addresses safety. If dance improvisation were, in fact, solely about one's own personal exploration and growth, then the chance for injury exponentially increases as additional bodies and objects are added into the space. I would argue (as I do later in this chapter) that it is specifically the improviser's ability to adapt to the constant change around them that makes for meaningful and mature work. While expanding one's own movement vocabulary is meaningful, doing so while remaining aware of one's surroundings not only provides for a much richer experience but also a safer one. As Wynton Marsalis said during an interview:

> Do I want to share the space? And that is what jazz (music) is really about. It's important to understand that you are sharing space with people who are not playing what you would play…but you can't stop in the middle of what you're playing and say 'don't play this, play what I would play'…how can I work with you in this space and find a way for us to swing.[2]

Dance Improvisation Is Neither Mystical Nor Sacred

One of the key phrases I hear over and over again when it comes to individuals who are unenthusiastic about taking another dance improvisation class is, "Are you going to make me be a tree again?" After I finish laughing internally (and sometimes out loud) when I am asked this question, I assure each person asking this question that my class is not that kind of class.

While some may be offended by a question such as this, I fully understand why this stereotype exists, and, to some extent, feel it is earned. After all, those of us who have been practicing dance improvisation for many years can, at times, get extremely theoretical about its nature and purpose. These conversations can sound philosophical due to the very real connections between the psychological state of a person's mind and the physical state of their body. Likewise, improvisers sometimes speak in terms of "trance, transformation, and flow," which can give the impression that a practitioner will (or must) reach an altered state in order to experience all that dance improvisation has to offer. However, despite these many attributes, dance improvisation is actually merely years of training and honing the body and mind in such a manner that the execution of spontaneous movement seems effortless, which, I would argue, is no different than any other form of dance training.

Improvisation Is Not Solely for Producing Choreography

While many longtime practitioners of dance improvisation may understand this concept, I still feel it necessary to address. Too often I have seen dance improvisation stand in as a mere tool for choreographic generation, rather than a legitimate dance technique which requires training, continued practice, and internal and external assessment. Perhaps this is because at its core, dance improvisation is about developing and enhancing one's own movement vocabulary. However, to merely reduce dance improvisation into a tool for creating choreography would be akin to training in tap dance merely to learn and execute choreography for a musical theater show. On the contrary, one pursues a lifetime of studying tap dance so that she/he/they might slowly begin to master self-expression, master rhythm, master musicality, and have shared experiences with other musicians/tap dancers, and, yes, repeat steps given to them by a choreographer with ease and effortlessness if needed. So too is it with dance improvisation.

What Is Improvisation?

It is also worth pausing for a moment to address the idea of assessment. Yes, dance improvisation can be assessed. After all, if it couldn't, then how would a practitioner know whether or not they were advancing in the study of it? Or, if dance improvisation couldn't be assessed, then how could an instructor give feedback to students as a means of demonstrating progress? While in its simplest form dance improvisation is about spontaneous movement generation, it is also about maturing as a moving, thinking, and physical being. Dance improvisation is about developing one's palate within the **Human Movement Buffet** and therefore must have some standards by which instructors and practitioners can distinguish growth from stagnation. It is, perhaps, because of this tension between self-discovery and practical evaluation that dance improvisation has at times been relegated to a mere choreographic tool.

Improvisation Is Not Doing Your Best Tricks

I will never forget my first introduction to the concept that dance improvisation is a spontaneous throw down of physical prowess. I was a recent college graduate, and I was auditioning for as many dance companies as possible with the hopes of landing a job. At one particular audition, I had made it through the entire 3-hour audition process and found myself to be one of the lucky and exhausted 10 individuals remaining in the dance studio. It was at this final portion of the audition that the director said the words that were like water to my dehydrated soul, "It's time to improvise."

I could literally feel myself exhale with a sigh of relief. I knew improvisation! I had spent the past three years taking every improvisation class I could find, attending every improve jam available, and had increasing my CD collection (yes, my CD collection!) to include every possible musical choice that didn't have counts. The last three hours of the audition had been filled with learning and regurgitating choreography, placing my body in someone else's movement world, and having to ensure that I could hit every accent and count required by the demonstrator. Finally, I would now have the opportunity to show "how I moved" and have the chance to acknowledge and engage with those remaining dancers in the room. I waited with eager anticipation to see what atmospheric music the company director would play as a way of setting the mood.

You can imagine to my surprise, then, when the director cranked up the volume on what I could only deduce was rave music: circa 1997. The director then instructed us to prepare 24 counts of "our best stuff," and we would each parade across the space executing a series of physical feats meant to elicit "oohs and aahs" of the people sitting behind the casting table. I was crushed and confused all at the same time. What was this new form of dance improvisation? Was this dance improvisation? And what in the world was I going to do in order to make up for the fact that I hadn't, until this point, developed 24 counts of my best stuff?

Hopefully you are, by now, laughing at my expense. Since that point in time, I have learned to embrace this sect of dance improvisation and can happily report that I now have more than 24 counts of my best stuff prepared when requested. However, I believe that in an attempt to make dance improvisation more accessible to young dancers, there is a very real danger in presenting it solely as a competitive event. Please don't misunderstand me, there is certainly nothing wrong with possessing the ability to throw down a sequence of awe-inspiring physical feats at any given time, but this alone does not capture the true essence and artistry that mastering dance improvisation can produce. Similarly, authentic dance improvisation takes into account the landscape, soundscape, needs and desires of those sharing the space, and an understanding of the desired outcome. Again, I am not saying that tricks cannot be dance improvisation, I am merely saying that they are a part of it and not the whole.

Improvisation Is Not Talent Based

This, above all other items, is perhaps why I love dance improvisation as a technique. While other dance forms require specific genetic traits in order to fully accomplish the physical demands and steps, dance improvisation always begins with the current state, both physical and mental, of the mover. It is, at its core, a truly equitable dance form. It accepts all movers, regardless of previous experience and training. It meets dancers and movers where they are. However, because of this, I many times see dancers with years of training in specific techniques struggle with dance improvisation. After all, they have spent years honing their bodies and minds to react in a manner that fits neatly within a codified theory/vocabulary. Likewise, I see young dancers dismiss dance improvisation as "dumb" or "trivial" because it does not give them the space to be superior. Dance improvisation is, perhaps, the most equitable of all dance forms.

Because of dance improvisation's inclusive nature, many teachers with whom I communicate are eager for their students to participate and grow in this dance form. However, they may struggle with how to teach it in a manner that is progression-based, accessible, and exciting. After all, if all are welcome, and skill is not the main outcome, then who is to say that not all are masters of dance improvisation from day one?

May I suggest that this conundrum stems from the primary and prevailing principle on which dance improvisation is based: there is no right or wrong (Chapter 2, Rule #1). For many individuals who have spent their entire professional careers training within the confines of a codified dance style or technique, the idea that there could be dance technique that is neither black nor white, but somehow still has a structure, is a concept that is, at best, unclear. After all, if there is no right or wrong, then how can we grade it? How do we give corrections? How can we teach it in a manner that encourages growth without stifling the enjoyment of play? How does a student progress from one level to another? Are there levels? What do we tell parents when they ask, "How's my child is doing in class?" What do we say to a student who says, "Why are we doing this?"

All of these questions are real and pertinent. The pressures of teaching our students new and exciting skills while remaining true to sound pedagogy is a fine balance. After all, there are only so many hours in a day and so many minutes in a dance class. Couple these struggles with the ever-present pressure of competition between local/neighboring dance studios, the ever-growing expansion of high school sports, and the travel and cost demands of dance competitions, we begin to realize that we must focus our efforts on those items that keep students returning to our classes and studios year after year. The great news is that there is room for both: new and exciting, and exploration.

So What Is Dance Improvisation?

Recognizing that I have not, as of yet, told you what dance improvisation is, I now divert our discussion from what it isn't to a more concrete (and perhaps more applicable) understanding of what dance improvisation is.

Dance improvisation, though philosophically complex and nuanced, is quite simple in its nature: it is a cycle. It is a cycle that, like laughter, feeds on itself as a means of sustaining. This cycle begins with an impulse. Later in this book (Chapter 4), I will discuss what an impulse truly is and is not, but for the sake of simplicity and time, let us simply agree that an impulse is the thing that causes one to act; and thus begins the cycle of improvisation. Once the impulse has struck, the dancer/mover then follows this impulse by acting upon it. By physically acting on the impulse, the dancer/mover has now changed the environment in which they exist. Similar to Newton's Third Law, for every action

What Is Improvisation?

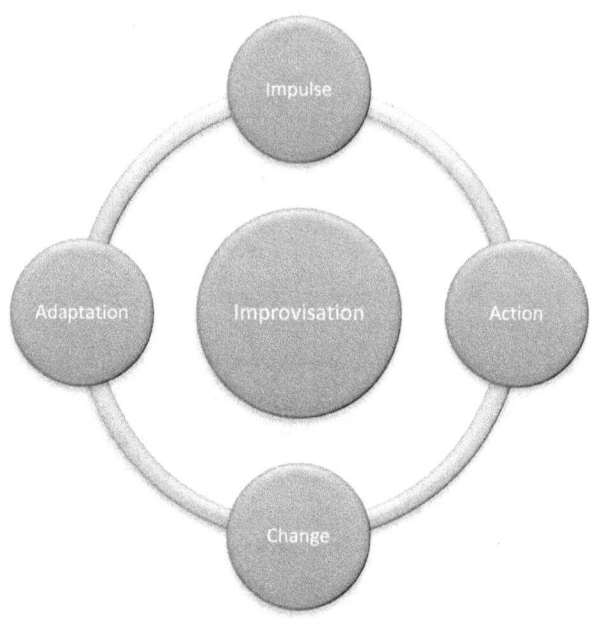

Figure 1.1 The Cycle of Improvisation

there is a separate but equal reaction. As the environment changes due to the action of the mover, the dancer/mover must now adapt to the change in environment; hence my conversation earlier that dance improvisation is not primarily a solo event. In adapting to the new environment, the dancer/mover opens him/her/themselves up to new impulses that arise. Thus, the cycle continues.

Figure 1.1 demonstrates this idea. I call this image the **Cycle of Improvisation**.

The beauty of this cycle is its simplicity. In naming this cycle I am attempting to remove the secrecy of dance improvisation and put it in a context that is much more relevant and comprehendible. This method of dance improvisation eliminates complexity and makes both the learning and teaching of dance improvisation something more translatable. Additionally, this system fits neatly within the many methods of dance improvisation (see Chapter 14) and therefore can assist in the teaching improvisation within almost all dance genres. In fact, fully understanding this model, you can now structure an entire course curriculum based on the whole cycle and its smaller, sub components.

Now that we understand what improvisation is, or at the very least, how it works, we can begin to build a foundation on which to construct our curriculum. This is where my *10 Rules of Improvisation: Plus 1* come into play. Each of these rules is a progression from the previous rule/rules, which ultimately leads the dancer/mover through a progression-based training program. While my methodology is meant to guide a dancer/mover to a finalized outcome, it is certainly not meant to serve as the end of the journey. Rather, these 11 rules are the keys to opening the door to a much larger and longer journey of dance improvisation. It is also worth noting that dance improvisation as spoken of in this book focuses on physical improvisation: specifically in the realm of contemporary dance. There are many other forms of improvisation (musical, visual, and auditory to name a few), and many other forms of dance improvisation within specific techniques. However, I would argue that the suggested physical entry point of this book makes the most sense for young dancers and movers. Once a true understanding and comfortability of physical improvisation is achieved, the other forms of improvisation are easily entered into via the transferable skills and ideas created through these 11 rules.

Considerations

Before we begin discussing theory, curriculum, progression, and exercises, let's pause for just a moment and try to answer the "ultimate question." You know, the one that every parent or principle will be asking you after the third or fourth week of introducing a dance improvisation curriculum into your studio or classroom. I am never offended or intimidated when people ask me this question, and neither should you be. After all, parents are spending their hard-earned money on dance classes and training for their child; and having their child take a class that has no trophy, final recital solo, or visible technical prowess may cause them to pause and wonder why this particular part of their child's training is necessary. To be honest, perhaps you yourself have asked this very same question. I know I have. What question am I referencing? Well.... it is simple, "Why does dance improvisation even matter?" Some individuals may bristle at this question, as if it is an affront to the technique and practice of this dance form. However, I delight in this question because it gives me the chance to explain all of the physical, mental, social, and artistic benefits of this specific dance form.

I have a dear friend and colleague who once said, "I have never deluded myself with the idea that dance would save the world – although I have always believed it makes the world a better place to save."[3] Her statement rings true for many aspects of our lives. However, for the sake of time, let me express that I too feel the same way about dance improvisation. Dance improvisation alone cannot save dance. If only it were that simple. However, dance without improvisation is not worth saving.

Suggesting that dance improvisation has no value because it has no trophies, final recital solo, or visible technical prowess are precisely the reasons why dance improvisation is so important. For starters, dancers who are eager practitioners of dance improvisation will tell you that their artistry, mental sharpness, and overall control of their physical instrument is dramatically improved due to their study and practice of improvisation. This, in turn (yes, I am going to say it), will lead to more trophies, a better senior recital solo, and enhanced physical prowess. While I understand that some may be aghast that I even brought these "low art" accomplishments into the discussion, it cannot be denied that these returns on investment are real and tangible benefits of studying dance improvisation. Additionally, why should we hide from the fact that dance improvisation does, in fact, have artistic, educational, physical, mental, and social benefits? Yes, it is so much more than a mere return on investment, but it equally produces some of the very same benefits that aid in winning dance competitions and landing a solo in the upcoming recital.

Epictetus (one of the great Stoics) wrote that "Man is not worried by real problems so much as by his imagined anxieties about real problems." While Stoics certainly wouldn't abide by some of the principles and ideas I will discuss in this book, I believe this quote gives great insight to the nature and source of much of the struggles we face as both dancers and people. More to the point, I believe what Epictetus is scratching (or perhaps digging) at what I perceive as the very real fear that many dancers (and humans) possess: the fear of immediacy and risk.

We as humans, and most certainly as dancers, fear risk and unpredictability because each represents the ultimate villain of performance: lack of control. We spend hours in classes and rehearsals perfecting our timing and steps. We also spend countless physical and mental hours perfecting our pre-show sequences, trying to grasp at every possible variable we can control: all in hopes of making the dance/performance as plannable and free of variables as possible. Yet, if we are honest with ourselves, it is all in pursuit of an idea that cannot be obtained: perfection. Therefore, rather than run away from the unknown, what if we could embrace it? Or, dare I say, what if we could master it?

The ability to master risk and immediacy, and engage with them in a manner that each becomes an ally rather than an enemy, is the ultimate pinnacle of dance improvisation. Suddenly, "performance quality" is no longer a veiled term shrouded in mystery and confusion. Artistry and creativity become readily accessible at our fingertips. Does this sound like an answer we can give our parents? Better yet, does this sound like a skill we want our students, or perhaps even ourselves, to possess?

If so, let us begin.

Citations

1 Farmer, Daniel. Father. 1951–Present.
2 Marsalis, Wynton, "The Democracy! Suite." Real Time with Bill Maher (HBO), 9 September 2022.
3 "Dance Part 1: An Antidote for Crazy Times." *YouTube*, uploaded by M.L. Graham, 25 October 2022, https:/Greeti/youtu.be/oUjlavdgXV0.

Notes

The 10 Rules of Improvisation; Plus 1

Introduction

With a basic understanding of what dance improvisation is and how it works, let's now turn our attention to the manner by which we can build a progression-based curriculum. This may, in fact, be precisely the reason you were drawn to this book.

Context

Rule #1 and Rule #2

Beginning our curricular foundation with Rule #1 (*There is No Right or Wrong...But Sometimes there is a Better Choice*) and Rule #2 (*Follow Your Impulse*), we can start to build our dance improvisation curriculum. These two rules are perhaps the most important and most difficult for trained dancers/movers to understand. They are also the two rules that take the most amount of time to master. For reasons I will discuss in further detail in Chapters 3 and 4, these two rules are where a majority of time is spent early on in improvisation training. These two rules are also continually revisited and reinforced throughout the curriculum. This section of foundational structure is all about games and exercises that expose students, ever so subtly, to the biases and predetermined ideas they possess that affect their understanding and approach to dance and movement. This is also the point at which the foundation of the class structure is set, as it mimics the feel and structure of a traditional dance studio course (i.e. warm-up, technique building exercises, across the floor, eventual center work, and combinations). This structure allows the students to feel comfortable, as it presents dance improvisation in a manner that is familiar to them. This, in turn, gives students the freedom to explore, try, and, most importantly, feel safe.

Rule #3 and Rule #4

Next in the program we move onto Rule #3 (*Start with What You Know*) and Rule #4 (*When in Doubt, Go Back to the Beginning*). With Rules #1 and #2 firmly comprehended, though not yet mastered, we can begin to explore the practice of putting ideas into motion. Until this point, I suggest students not even begin to thinking about, let alone actually start, what they perceive as "dance improvisation." During this period of the course structure, I limit the amount of time spent in a dance improvisation, and I always ensure that any dance improvisation introduced is always at the end of class (i.e. the "combination") and guided by the instructor. Additionally, any dance improvisation occurring at this point in the curriculum is either a solo affair, or, at most, a duet. Lastly, any dance improvisation that takes place during this part of the curriculum is an expansion of an existing exercise, and never a standalone event. In other words, it is not yet time to set sail and "improvise." Rather, it is merely time to step onto the proverbial ship and begin to develop our sea legs – all the while remaining safe in port.

Rule #5 and Rule #6

Venturing into Rule #5 (*The Moment You Check Out, Someone Gets Hurt*) and Rule #6 (*It Takes a Village to Raise an Improvisation*), this is the very first time I introduce the idea (yes…only the idea) of group improvisation. Up until this point, improvisational work (again, always at the end of class) has either been a solo or duet affair. In this portion of my curricular scaffolding, I begin to introduce the idea of "touch" (i.e. students making physical contact with one another). I do not allow students to physically touch one another at any point during class until this point in the curriculum, and even then, I simply introduce the idea of touch. There are several class periods, sometimes weeks, dedicated solely to the introduction of the idea and practice of physical contact, which includes discussing and unpacking the cultural biases and baggage we all harbor surrounding touch. We also discuss consent during this portion of the curriculum.

I will dive into touch further in Chapter 7, but for now, physical contact is simply introduced and explored on a very elementary level. I also begin the introduction of larger group improvisations around this same time.

Rule #7 and Rule #8

Rule #7 (*The Hardest Part Isn't Knowing When to Start, It's Knowing How to Start*) and Rule #8 (*Everything You Need Exists in the World Around You*) is where I begin to introduce students to group improvisations outside of exercises, as well as the shape and intention behind improvisation as a performance art form. By this point in the curriculum, students are comfortable with recognizing their own personal movement biases, exploring their own non-natural, internal impulse (more about this in Chapter 4), and improvising without the need of verbal guidance from the instructor. Up until this point, dance improvisations have always begun with guidance and instruction, but this is the first time students are allowed to enter into a group improvisation on their own: no guidelines, no coaching, and no set outcomes. In other words, we are, for the first time, allowing students to raise the anchor and sail out of port on their own. However, as a means of continued growth, I start encouraging students to look for external stimulus as an impulse point, and not just their own internal inklings.

Rule #9 and Rule #10

Heading into the final stretch of my curricular approach, students should, by this time, be feeling the flow of dance improvisation. They can now improvise in a larger group setting for quite some time. However, using our sailing metaphor, it is at this point that students know just enough to get themselves into danger but not enough to get themselves out of it. Because of this, you may notice that, like Christmas morning, dance improvisations in class will be highly anticipated, with much joy and excitement surrounding them. However, also like Christmas morning, the students will hurriedly open all of their "gifts" (i.e. try everything you have done in class thus far), but in doing so quickly run out of steam.

Therefore, it is at this level of our progression pyramid that I introduce two very helpful and necessary tools: Mapping and Stillness (Rule #9: *Continual Movement in and of itself is not Improvisation*). The tools learned in this section of the curriculum, along with a greater self-awareness of the "arc" of an improvisation, will allow your students to begin to grasp and execute the full power of dance improvisation. Ultimately, it is here (again to use our sailing analogy) that we help them guide and chart their own course by seeing the best possible passageways, while avoiding troubled waters (Rule #10: *Be Wary of the Black Hole*).

Plus 1 (Rule #11)

The pinnacle of my curricular pyramid ends with Rule #11 or what I call "Plus 1." By this point in the students' training, they have mastered (I use this word loosely, as mastery takes a lifetime) the previous 10 rules, and they are able to comprehend and apply all 10 rules on command. However, as with the previous levels of our curriculum, there are pitfalls into which the students may stumble. The main pitfall is that dance improvisations could, in theory, continue on forever. After all, improvisation is a cyclical event and therefore has no "real" ending; it is quite literally the song that never ends. However, who wants to actually watch that?

The other pitfall I see students encounter at this point is the thought that "new is always better." Students mistakenly think that improvisation is merely the creation of new movement and never repeats itself. On the contrary, master performance improvisers exist in a world between spontaneous movement generation and movement recall: all in pursuit of creating a cohesive and engaging experience.

Lastly, it is also at this stage in the process where I remind students of the previous 10 rules and reinforce the necessity for continual practice. It is imperative that we as teachers begin to speak of dance improvisation in the same vocabulary as other dance techniques. Just as we encourage our students to continue practice of their dance skills outside of class, so too do we need to encourage the practice of dance improvisation.

The pyramid graph shows that there is a logical and applicable progress to the education and practice of dance improvisation. This scaffold process allows us to build curriculum for the various age groups we teach in our studios, as well as a curriculum that sustains not just over weeks and months, but over years. This being said, certainly not all age groups are meant to learn or practice each level of the pyramid. I certainly would not expect children at the age of 5 to even begin discussing, let alone comprehending, any of the upper

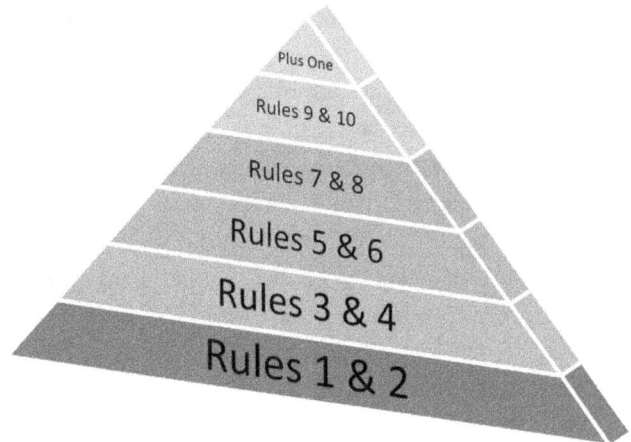

Figure 2.1 Curricular Pyramid

philosophical ideas and practices of this pyramid. However, creative dance for children's classes is an excellent way to introduce young dancers to the concept of creative and expressive movement that has no predetermined right or wrongness. Additionally, I wouldn't encourage middle school-aged students to address some of the headier concepts discussed and explored in the later chapters. However, the groundwork and exploration of the lower pyramid concepts can certainly occur through some of the exercises discussed in this book, as well as by making dance improvisation as common in your studio curriculum as many other dance forms you offer. Above all, it is about consistency and normalcy. To quote my father once again, "If a leader truly believes in something, then he/she will lead by example."

Considerations

Before we dive into these individual rules, there is one additional item I would like to address: Guidelines for Engagement. Without addressing this item, we run a very real risk of our classes and students falling into apathy, at best, or chaos, at worst. These two extremes occur due to normal student behavior:

a) Laughter due to uncomfortableness
b) Frustration with length of progress
c) Lack of engagement due to fear

By addressing these challenges at the beginning of the process, you set the ground rules by which your students will engage. Again, I bring it back to other dance classes. Just like all other dance forms have their class etiquette requirements, so too does dance improvisation.

The following list is certainly not an exhaustive one (please feel free to add to it as you grow in your teaching of dance improvisation), but it is a good starting place meant to keep your students focused and respectful. I will break down each of these briefly, but for now, read them, re-read them, and perhaps think what you can pull from your other class experiences in order to make connections.

Guidelines for Class Engagement

1. What Happens in Class, Stays in Class
2. Creativity Cannot Exist in a World without Trust
3. Trust the Process
4. Laughter is Okay – Just Not at Each Other
5. Try First, Ask Second
6. Take Your Time
7. The Instructor Must be an Active Participant

What Happens in Class, Stays in the Class

This, above all other guiding principles for class etiquette, is perhaps the most important. There is a tendency we have as humans: the need to talk about new experiences. This is a wonderful thing and should be encouraged by always leaving time during and at the end of class in order for discussion to occur. However, many students will also want to chat about what occurred in class at home, at school, and, worst case scenario, online. Encourage your students to keep all conversation surrounding class exercises, occurrences, and on-goings within class discussion. This serves two purposes. Frist, it allows all students to participate freely without the worry of their actions being discussed in an inappropriate manner outside of your purview. We would never want a situation to arise where a student is either bullied or made fun of in a manner that could very possibly stretch across the globe via social media. Secondly, keeping the class details within the classroom setting prevents individuals from outside of the class (parents, other students, community members, etc.) from making or passing judgment without the full context of every situation.

Creativity Cannot Exist in a World without Trust

For reasons that are obvious, the first Guideline for Class Engagement fits neatly within the dance studio atmosphere. Students who do not feel safe to try and explore without judgment will never reach, or even scratch the surface of, their creative potential. In addition to trust needing to be built outside the dance studio/classroom (i.e. What happens in class stays in class), trust must also be built within the walls of the studio. Students must understand that trust, or dare I say vulnerability, is inherent in the creative process: particularly in dance improvisation. Therefore, anything said or done during class that breaks that trust also breaks the ability to learn and grow. Students will need to be made aware of, and become comfortable with, trusting their fellow classmates. By learning to trust and be trusted, your students will unlock the fullest potential of each class and themselves.

Trust the Process

It is inevitable that at some point during a class, or the course of the curriculum, every single student will ask, "Why are we doing this?" Perhaps you'll ask yourself this same question. This is a great question with many answers. However, like all codified dance techniques, there comes a time where every student has to trust the process. The beginning tap dance student may wonder why they always have to practice shuffles so many times. Similarly, the intermediate, and even the advanced, ballet student will at times inquire the need for so many plies.

In all of these situations, we as teachers understand that the students' progress, strength, longevity, and safety all lie within the long-term process. The same can be said for dance improvisation. Those of us new to dance improvisation may at times wonder, "Why am I being asked to do this?" Meanwhile, those of us who have participated dance improvisation for quite some time may be asking, "Why can't I break the rules?" In both instances, I encourage you and your students to trust the process. As mentioned, this is not a blind trust I ask of you; dance improvisation is not mysticism or faith. Rather, it is an agreement to see the whole curriculum through before deciding if the view was worth the journey.

Laughter Is Okay – Just Not at Each Other

Laughter is inevitable during exploration and new environments. It is a way for the human body and psyche to release tension that builds up due to discomfort or cognitive dissonance. Therefore, do not shut down laughter from your students when it is being expressed in a manner that is helpful, appropriate, and specifically directed at themselves. This helps to ensure that dance improvisation doesn't become a tedious, joyless experience. However, do make sure your students understand that laughing at others during class is unacceptable. As mentioned before, no student, or human for that matter, can feel free to explore and make mistakes if they are deterred by the fear of embarrassment. As the old saying goes, "I can make fun of my family, but nobody else can." In other words, there is a healthy dose of humility and freedom in being allowed to laugh at oneself but never freedom in being laughed at.

Try First, Ask Second

You may have already run into this in your other dance classes (or perhaps I am alone in experiencing this), but I am seeing a trend with young dancers: they want to understand everything about a particular step or situation before they try it. Because of this, I tend to see students ask millions of questions. I will leave the reasons behind this trend to social psychologists and sociologists. Regardless of the reasons, this trend presents some challenges when it comes to dance improvisation, and life for that matter.

The first challenge is there is no way anyone can understand something fully before engaging with it. After all, that is the point of trying something new. While a healthy bit of skepticism and understanding is always welcome, eventually there comes a time in dance (and life) where one must take a leap of faith. Ultimately, dance improvisation is about the new, the unknown, and the yet to be discovered. Therefore, I encourage you to remind your students to try first and ask questions second. Or, to put it differently, "don't get bogged down in the details."

Take Your Time

One of the reasons I feel that dance improvisation has failed to take hold in dance studios and classrooms across the country is because of a larger cultural influence (perhaps one that you are already aware of) in the United States. It's the idea that production is the same as progress. For too long, young dancers, and their parents, have bought into the idea that as long as there is a tangible product at the end of an experience (be it a trophy, a t-shirt, or a sweaty body), then surely progress in their training has been made. I am sure you have experienced this same frustration. How many of our students have decided to not take that extra dance class because they've decided that volleyball, soccer, cheerleading, dance team, or some other extracurricular activity was "more rewarding." Don't misunderstand me, I myself played sports in high school and feel there is very much a place for all physical activities in the development of a young person. However, the immediate nature of "winner versus loser," and the instant gratification of "scoring a point, or beating the other team," has assisted the idea that if an activity doesn't have immediate results, then it surely must not be worth the time investment.

This is the challenge with dance improvisation and all dance for that matter. Immediate gratification rarely exists, and slow, incremental, and, many times, uncomfortable growth is the norm. Therefore, as you begin to build and execute your dance improvisation curriculum, please remember that, like fine wine, the process should be slow, detailed, and intentional. The fruits of the labor come months, if not years, later, but oh what wonderful fruit it is.

The Instructor Must Be an Active Participant

One of the biggest misconceptions about teaching dance improvisation is that instruction somehow falls outside the bounds of best pedagogical practice, and that the instructor is a passive observer. On the contrary, as the captain of this proverbial ship, the instructor must be willing to lead the way in demonstrating play, laughing at oneself, keeping a watchful eye for ways to adapt the class in real-time, finding teachable movements, and creating a safe environment where students feel the freedom to try, flop, and try again.

It is imperative that the instructor be willing to adapt the class structure, its exercises, and/or the questions posed during discussion instantaneously based on what she/he/they are witnessing. This is no different from how we as teachers adjust the structure in our other dance classes: by slowing things down, repeating some exercises multiple times, and/or completely changing the structure of the class based on the immediate needs of the students.

In this book, I will supply suggested questions to prompt conversation, but ultimately, it is up to each instructor to choose which questions are best, or to throw my suggested questions out and come up with completely new questions/prompts based on what you are observing. Remember, you have years of experience behind you, and teaching dance improvisation is merely an extension of your expertise.

Try

Exercises for Introduction to Dance Improvisation (i.e. Dipping Your Toe in the Water)

This first exercise was taught to me by an instructor in graduate school during our improvisation course. I love this exercise for several reasons:

1) Regardless of a dancer's training, it puts everyone on an equal playing field.
2) It literally follows the cycle of improvisation.
3) All of my *10 Rules of Improvisation: Plus 1* apply to this exercise in a manner that is easy to understand and is progressive in nature.

Juggling

For full instructions and visual assistance on how to learn to juggle, you can perform a simple internet search. However, here are some additional tips and tricks in order to make the process more enjoyable and progress-based:

- While students can roll up two pairs of socks to make juggling objects, I usually recommend hacky sacks: three to be exact. Hacky sacks have more weight, and their pliability makes them easier to control. Plus, unlike tennis balls, hacky sacks don't bounce all over the studio when dropped. Silk scarves are also a nice alternative, as they float longer in the air – giving your students more time to process the actions and timing needed for juggling.
- Have your right-handed students start with a singular juggling item in their left hand. Have your left-handed students start with a singular juggling item in their right hand.
- Have your students stand in a circle and practice tossing the juggling object up in the air and catching it with the same hand. Once they have mastered this,

have them continue to stand in a circle and practice tossing the juggling object up in the air and catching it with the same hand without looking directly at the object or their hand. They must start to engage their peripheral vision.
- Once this is mastered, have the students begin walking around the room practicing the same exercise. Be sure to instruct them to look into the eyes of the people they are passing and say "Hello." This will prevent your students from focusing their gaze solely on the juggling object and their hand.
- Once the previous exercise has been mastered – add a second juggling item. This item is held in the other hand so that each hand is holding a juggling item.
    - Have the students stand in a circle.
    - Start from the beginning of this exercise.
    - Students will toss one juggling item in the air and catch it in the same hand. The next step is to toss the second juggling item in the air and catch it with the same hand that just tossed it.
    - Follow the same progression as you did with the singular juggling item and then have your student begin to walk around the room. Again, remind them to look at those around them and say "hello" as they pass by.
- Go back to the beginning with the students forming a circle.
    - This time have your students toss the first juggling item in the air and catch it in the other hand. This of course means that they will need to toss the second juggling item before catching the first juggling item.
    - The phrase I use here is "Toss, Toss – Catch, Catch."
    - Repeat the entire progression again (Standing in a circle, standing in a circle but not looking directly at the juggling items or the hands, walking around, and walking around and saying "Hello").
- Once mastered, students can now add the third juggling item. Refer to any YouTube video that teaches juggling.
    - Once again, start from the beginning of the process and slowly increase what the students are doing as they practice their juggling skills.
- I use the many steps and progressions of this warm-up for the first 5 minutes of every improvisation class I teach. This initial warm-up lasts for the 2–3 weeks, if the class meets 3 days per week. You can plan and adjust as needed based on how many days your students meet for improvisation class.

- Ultimately, the key is not to rush from one section of this exercise to the next too quickly. Take your time. The single hand toss and catch can easily last several classes as the initial warm-up.

Walking Exercise

I use this exercise with all levels because it is a great full-body warm-up and introduces students to the idea that improvisation is neither scary, nor as serious as we sometimes make it.

- Instruct your students to begin walking around the space. As they do so, they are to look at one another as they pass. As they continue to walk, the idea is to **not** run into one another but rather avoid making physical contact. They should remain focused but loose, aware, and yet adaptive.

Walking Exercise #1

As the exercise continues, have your students pick up the pace by first walking faster (approximately 2–3 minutes), then jogging (approximately 1–2 minutes), and finally running (approximately 90 seconds).

- Again, the entire idea is to <u>avoid</u> contact/collision, thus introducing the students to the idea of "action and re-action."
- As they get warm, reverse the speed from running, to jogging, to a fast walk, and finally walking.
- Once the students have returned to walking, instruct them to pause for a moment (i.e. when they feel the impulse) and then continue walking again. In doing this, you are having the students improvise without their knowledge. In other words, they are following an impulse, changing the environment around themselves, adapting/adjusting to that environmental change, and then following a new impulse based on this change. It is, quite literally, the cycle of improvisation.

You will see this exercise in later chapters, but for now, allow this exercise to remain simple and clear.

Like juggling, I use this exercise as the second warm-up for my improvisation classes. It lasts approximately 5–8 minutes and occurs every class for several weeks.

Walking Exercise #2

Instruct your students to walk around the room. After you allow the students to walk around the room for a bit, bring them back to the circle you formed for the juggling exercise.

- Ask your students this simple question: "What were you instructed to do?" Through various answers they will come to the conclusion that they were asked to walk around the room. If they do not get to this answer, then softly guide them to this conclusion.
- Once they have come to this conclusion, now ask them, "Did you, in fact, walk AROUND the room?" This will (ideally) open up dialogue for discovery of biases and habits. For example:
  1. Did the students walk around the room, or just in the middle of the dance studio? If they remained mostly in the middle of the studio, ask them why?
  2. Did the students walk around the studio, or did they eventually all begin walking in the same direction (i.e. in a circle around the studio)? If they eventually began walking all in the same direction, ask them why?
  3. Did the students walk around the studio facing forward the entire time (i.e. their faces where always leading them through space), or did they explore walking backward and sideways? If they walked forward most of the time, ask them why?

Questions and observations such as these introduce the students to the idea that they have been "pre-programmed" to behave in a manner that is deemed appropriate for their culture and society. They are completely unaware that they are making daily choices (such as walking) that they believe are their own, but are, in all honesty, someone else's.

- Armed with this knowledge, have your students begin to walk around the room again. You could also, should you choose, have them walk around following each individual question. I personally prefer the second option, as it allows the student to process one new piece of information, rather than trying to process multiple pieces of information.

- After some time, have the students return to the conversation circle once again. It is time for more observations and questions:
  1. Did the students remain vertical and erect while walking around, or did they explore levels? If they remained standing while walking, ask them why?
  2. If the students did explore levels, were their feet always touching the ground? If their feet were always touching the ground, ask them why?
  3. Did the students fall into a walking cadence/rhythm that eventually had them all walking in time with one another? If they fell into the same cadence, ask them why?

Repeat this exercise again, armed with even more information. Feel free to repeat this exercise as many times as you desire, looking for ways in which your students fall privy to cultural and social norms that dictate what it means to "walk," what it means to "explore," and what it means to simply be in a dance studio (for example – continually referencing oneself in the mirror).

After each walking exercise, be sure to come back to the conversation circle in order to ask questions, arm the students with new information, and begin again.

Walking Exercise #3

This walking exercise should be reserved for later in the curriculum, as it requires the students to understand that the command to walk around the studio need not fall in the context of what the general American society deems appropriate for walking. This being said, do not wait too long to introduce it, as it is a great strength-building exercise.

- Instruct the student to walk around the room. After a few minutes, instruct them to now bear crawl.
  - In case you are unfamiliar with a bear crawl, it is a manner of moving through space where both hands and both feet are in contact with the floor, and the backside of the body is facing upward.

- Be sure to emphasize the need to bear crawl in a manner where the students' knees do not touch the floor, and that their same arm and leg move together, as opposed to the opposite arm and the opposite leg moving simultaneously.
- After several minutes of bear crawling, have the students return to walking. Instruct them to "play" (i.e. transition) between walking and bear crawling.
  - Allow this to continue for several more minutes.
- As the students become comfortable with this process, you can now add another animal movement: the crab crawl.
  - Instruct your students to begin making their way through space with a crab crawl.
  - In case you are unfamiliar with the crab crawl, it is a manner of moving through space where both feet and both hands are in contact with the floor, but the front half of the body is facing upward.
  - Be sure to emphasize need to ensure that the students' hips are pressing toward the sky.
- After several minutes of crab crawling, have the students return to a bear crawl and then to walking.
  - Instruct the students to play (i.e. transition) between walking, bear crawling, and crab crawling: ensuring that the transition between each is smooth and seamless.
- As the students become comfortable with this process, you can now add a third animal movement: the monkey crawl.
  - Instruct your students to begin making their way through space with a monkey crawl.
  - In case you are unfamiliar with a monkey crawl, it is merely moving through space in a low squatted position, where the hands are used to assist movement through space (i.e. think of how an ape move through space).
  - Students can also perform physical tasks in this section such as knee slides, small hand stands, and any other manner of movement that reflects how monkeys move.
- After several minutes of monkey crawling, have the students return to a crab crawl, then a bear crawl, and then to walking.

- Instruct the students to play between walking, bear crawling, crab crawling, and monkey crawling.
- Remind them that the transition between each should be smooth and seamless.
- As the students become comfortable with this process, you can now add a final animal movement: the lizard crawl.
  - Instruct your students to begin making their way through space with a lizard crawl.
  - In case you are unfamiliar with a lizard crawl, it is a manner of moving through space where both feet and both hands are in contact with the floor, the front portion of the body is facing the floor, and the chest, stomach, and hips are no more than 3–4 inches away from the ground.
  - This locomotive task requires a large amount of upper body and core strength, and therefore, students may not be able to remain in this movement phase for long periods of time. However, encourage them to continually push themselves to remain in the lizard crawl as long as possible. This will build both mental and physical strength.
- After a minute or so of lizard crawling, have the students return to a monkey crawling, then crab crawling, followed by bear crawling, and finally to walking.
  - Instruct the students to play between walking, bear crawling, crab crawling, monkey crawling, and lizard crawling, ensuring that the transition between each is smooth and seamless.

This entire walking exercise can, and I would argue should, evolve over multiple classes, if not weeks. There is no reason to rush to try and get to lizard crawl in a singular class, or even five classes for that matter. Remember, we are just introducing our students to the idea of alternative locomotive actions, and spending more time in a particular area will build comfort, strength, and creativity.

Walking Exercise #4

This walking exercise is a great extension of Walking Exercise #1 and continues the idea of mind/body agency as it relates to students making decisions within established guidelines.

The 10 Rules of Improvisation; Plus 1

- Instruct your students to begin walking around the space.
    - As with Walking Exercise #1, remind the students that it is okay for this exercise that they remain vertical and upright while walking.
    - After several minutes of walking around, instruct the students to begin exploring their "Belly, Back, and Bottom/Butt" specifically in this order.
    - There will undoubtedly be some looks and questions regarding what you mean by this statement. This is okay because it provides the ideal time to remind students of one of the rules of engagements – Try first. Ask second.
- As the students begin to grapple with and explore this concept (Belly, Back, Butt), instruct them to begin walking again.
    - Now that they have had one attempt at this exploration, you can now begin to have them play with transitioning between walking and exploring their "Belly, Back, and Bottom/Butt." This time, however, tell them that they simply need to pass through all three areas before walking again.
    - You will also want to remind them to change the ways in which they explore these three areas, continue to work on smooth transitions between each, as well as find unique and alternative ways in which to go to the floor and rise up out of it.

This exercise can continue as long as desired. You can also alter the exercise later by adjusting the speed at which the students are walking and exploring, adding or subtracting body parts, and/or having the students find an alternative mode of moving through space (i.e. Walking Exercise #3).

As with the previous walking exercises, take time with each new introduction. This initial exercise can exist over multiple classes before a new tempo, body part, or additional task is introduced. I will stress this point throughout the book: **racing to the end is not the goal! Take your time.**

Notes

Rule #1 – There Is No Right or Wrong… But Sometimes There Is a Better Choice

Introduction

Before we begin exploring exercises and ideas surrounding students' ideas of right vs. wrong (often times reflected in their physical choices when moving), it is worth taking a moment to better understand how these ideas of right vs. wrong are imbedded within their psyche via culture, society, and, yes, some dance training itself. A better understanding of "How we got here" will not only guide us into forming exercises and practices that can better serve our students, but it will also assist us in becoming better teachers and people. Let us first address how the simple concept of right vs. wrong has impacted all of us (students and teachers alike) both as humans and dancing artists.

Context

Arguments and discussions regarding right vs. wrong have been ongoing since the dawn of philosophical thought. Everyone from the ancient Greeks, to the Persians, to modern-day song writers has tried to tackle the meaning between what is right and what is wrong. For the sake of brevity, let me first address that this chapter will in no way try to answer the eternal question of, "What is Right and What is Wrong?" After all, these philosophical conversations can go in many directions and can span all subjects from morality and ethics to history, religion, sex, and politics. Likewise, there are great questions such as "right and wrong according to who," and "right vs wrong based on what benefit?" We could very much get lost in the weeds when trying to tackle this idea, and therefore, we will leave the greater discussion and debate to philosophers, social scientist,

DOI: 10.4324/9781003387084-4

historians, and (sparingly) politicians. Instead, let us simply look at how right and wrong expose themselves in our lives and in dance.

Richard Rohr discusses in many of his writings the idea of "Non-dualistic Thinking."[1] In the current context, we might call this non-binary thinking, or the ability to see the world in terms of both-and, rather than This or That. While this may not sound like a radical idea, it actually runs completely counter to most experiences many people have in their lives. Binary thinking is pervasive in American culture, and its manifestation exists in almost every nook and cranny. When sitting at a stop sign, the two options are to "Stop" or "Go." When we meet someone for the first time, we many times classify them into historic gender roles (male or female). We may also do this with race, economic status (rich or poor), and a host of other binary descriptors that allow us to determine someone's identity as it relates to their differences between us and them (big vs small, short vs tall, pretty vs plain, pleasant vs. dangerous, etc.).

This segmentation of our world into "This or That" doesn't end with interactions between our fellow humans. American political parties (Republican vs Democrat), general faith practices (religious vs non-religious, spiritual or not spiritual), the education system (college vs trades), the cars we drive (Honda vs Ford), the clothes we wear (chic vs boho), the way we view ourselves (attractive vs ugly), and even our very first steps on this planet (walk vs. crawl) are all a result of trying to classify the world into tidy distinctions. From the very earliest stages of a child's life, we begin to initiate them into a world of binary thinking: we first encourage them to crawl, but then suddenly that isn't good enough, and now, they must walk – ergo, walking is right/better and crawling is wrong/worse. This or That.

Because of this saturation of right vs. wrong, we grow up learning to stifle what little independence and creativity remains. We spend our lives ensuring that we fall within the societal and cultural norms that are deemed appropriate (right), all the while avoiding chances, opportunities, risks, and moments that might bring unwanted social attention/embarrassment to ourselves (wrong). So, what then is the effect of this on our students as moving artists? Well, ask yourself how many classes a dance student takes in a given day, and how many of those classes are based on a set of right and wrong rules. The answer you may have come to is all of them or at least most of them. After all, even when teaching ballet class, I tell my students all of the time, "a tendu, is a tendu, is a tendu…. either it is, or it isn't." Did you catch that? Either it is right or it is wrong. I would argue that this example is not limited to ballet class (though ballet of all dance forms is quite codified in its rightness and wrongness) but occurs throughout many dance technique classes. Whether it is the "right" way to do a shuffle in tap or the "wrong way" to execute a leap in jazz. There is the right way to groove in Hip Hop, and the wrong way to do a contraction in modern. Our dance students are saturated from the time they wake up to the time they go to bed with a never-ending list of what is the right way to do things and what is the wrong way to do them. This then leads us to the challenge of creativity.

The problem is not that our students aren't creative, it's that they are rarely given a structured and dedicated time under which creative exploration and freedom are the main goals. There is little time in their dance training (let alone their daily life) where their mistakes, creativity, and imaginations are encouraged to flourish and prosper. Rather, they spend hours per day learning and relearning the "correct" manner by which they will become a "better" student, dancer, and person. There it is again: the word "better." This word alone inherently informs our students that there is obviously the counter option (i.e. worse), and since better is better, there must be only one "right" path to become better.

The inherent effect of all of this rightness and wrongness is that our students are great at reproducing what is given to them but struggle when presented with a situation where there may be more than one correct option. Sir Ken Robinson discusses this idea in several of his speeches found online. In his various presentations, he argues that skills such as independence, creativity, imagination, and lateral thinking have been pushed out of school curriculum and replaced by the more societally acceptable, and dare I say lucrative, abilities of conformity, regurgitation, and linear thinking. This ever-advancing movement toward STEM (Science, Technology, Engineering, and Math), and not STEAM (Science, Technology, Engineering, **Arts**, and Math), has pushed many students to the educational margins simply because their talents lie in areas outside of the educational and social norms. One could argue that many forms of dance training in the United States today have behaved in a similar fashion.

Is it no wonder then, based on the enormous tidal wave that our students face, that they struggle with spontaneous individual creativity? How many times have you found yourself frustrated as recital season, competition season, or Nutcracker seasons comes around that your dance students are executing all of the steps given to them with flawless implementation but are yet missing that "special spark?" The answer is, I assume, at least yearly.

The question we must then ask ourselves is, "Why would our students understand such items as originality and personal creativity if little of their consistent training prepares them for this?" In truth, there is not much in today's performance-focused dance training, with perhaps the exception of combinations at the end of class, where dance students are trained to tap into something deeper than the reparative execution of steps. Is it any wonder that dance forms such as Hip Hop and tap, which are founded in improvisation, personal expression, and flare, are the fastest growing trends among today's youth?

Please don't misunderstand me. I am by no means diminishing historic performance-focused dance training and the need for continued and anatomically correct preparation. On the contrary, it is only through repetition that the body is able to master physical execution and prowess. However, I am advocating that in the same way many place an emphasis on repetitive and continued study of specified techniques as a means to ensure proper physical execution, vocabulary, and body mastery, we as educators also need to emphasize repetitive and continued training in creativity, personal choice/voice, and spontaneity.

Understanding the wave of binary thinking that inundates our world, and the gap that exists in much of our students' training, we can now see that young dancers are rarely given a purposeful and dedicated opportunity to explore and build upon their own personal creativity and artistry. So, how do we begin to change this? The answer is by tackling Rule #1 of my 11 Rules for Improvisation: *There is No Right or Wrong…But Sometimes There Is a Better Choice*. This rule, along with Rule #2, *Follow You Impulse*, will consume a vast majority of the early dance improvisation training for your dancers. In a given college semester (15 weeks), I will spend the first 4 weeks (meeting three times per week – i.e. Mondays, Wednesdays, and Fridays – for 1.5 hours each class) working on just these two ideas. After all, understanding that right and wrong are ingrained in our dancers, it only makes sense that one quarter of their training would be dedicated to undoing 12–16 years of social training.

Considerations

Before diving into the recommended exercises, let me also point out the fact that Rule #1 actually consists of two parts. I have spent a large amount of time thus far discussing the first portion, *There is No Right or Wrong*, but I haven't spent time addressing the second half of the rule, *…But Sometimes There is a Better Choice*. The second half of this rule may seem contradictory to the first part, but in all actuality, it works well with the preceding discussion in this chapter. The second half of this rule is all about safety.

As you continue to press your students to take risks and break all the rules of society, you will, at some point, need to discuss with them the idea of physical, emotional, and mental safety. For me, the "better" choice as related to the rule is always based on the physical, mental, and emotional safety of my students. Therefore, while there is not a "right and wrong" when it comes to movement exploration, physical harm will inevitably lead down a path that is both destructive and harmful. Therefore, whenever students are practicing exercises, and eventually improvising, be sure to continually guide them in a manner that emphasizes creativity, while simultaneously ensuring safety for all participants. As I say to my students when I teach improvisation, "You may choose to throw yourself out that window during and improvisation because there is no 'right or wrong,' but it will be the first and last time you throw yourself out that window since we are on the second story of this building." As morbid as this example sounds, it drives home the idea that "right and wrong" apply only to the artistic and creative world and not the world of physics, gravity, and bodily health.

Let me also acknowledge that not all dance forms focus purely on right and wrong. After all, in some historic teaching methods of tap, jazz, and Hip Hop, improvisation is an integral part of the training and the product. However, while incorporating dance improvisation as a part of the training, these dance forms still have structured outcomes that guide and mold how dance improvisation should be used. Therefore, I would like to make the argument that it is our ability to see how dance improvisation can benefit all dance teaching methods that limits our students' ability to be spontaneous creative beings. I would also like to suggest that many teachers have traditionally classified dance technique in a manner that limits our students' ability to understand a dance environment where right and wrong is secondary to creativity and spontaneity.

With these ground rules now in place, let us explore several exercises that are meant to assist your students in learning how to break out of their right and wrong mindsets.

Try

Exercise #1: Wiggling

This exercise is designed to aid students in becoming comfortable with the uncomfortable. The premise is quite simple and is a great introduction to moving through space.

Instruct the students to stand at one end of the studio. Have three to four of them step forward to form a line (think getting ready to do progressions across the floor). The rest of the students line up behind one of the lead students.

Rule #1 – There Is No Right or Wrong

The first line is now going to travel from one side of the room to the other. However, in order to do so, each student must throw a singular body part forward into space, thus allowing the force of that limb to advance them through space. The resulting effect of this exercise is that the students will appear to wiggle through space, one appendage at a time.

Remind the students of several items:

- They should not travel any further than makes sense for the amount of force generated by the single appendage being tossed. In other words, if I toss my arm into space, it would make little sense for me to travel 8–12 steps in reaction; seeing that my arm by no means has the force or weight to pull/throw my entire body that distance. Rather, I may, at best, take a step or two.
- There are more than four appendages (two arms and two legs): remind them to use their heads as well.
- Allow them to toss forward at first but then challenge them to toss backward and sideways.
- As students progress, challenge them to change up their timing and speed with which they toss and react.
- After some time, you can encourage your students to toss two appendages at the same time and react to this new sensation.
- You may also expand what is being tossed into space. Rather than limit the exercise to appendages, you may eventually choose to allow students to "throw" any body part into the space. For example, perhaps they try to "throw" their right ear into space as a means of movement generation, or perhaps their elbow or their 6th rib bone.
- Have fun with expanding your students understanding of their own body parts as they advance in this exercise. Be creative but also push them to be specific.

Exercise #2: Run, Stop, Change/Change…Run, Stop, Clap with Change/Change…and Run, Stop, Clap/Clap with 2 Half-Turns

This exercise was introduced to me by Professor Steven Iannacone[2] early in my training, and it has remained with me throughout these many years, particularly for three reasons:

Rule #1 – There Is No Right or Wrong

1. The simplicity of this exercises ensures that all students (no matter how physically talented they may be) will struggle with it the first (and even second and third) try.
2. It demonstrates almost immediately that this technique class will be different, and therefore, it is time to change one's perspective of how to excel in class.
3. This exercise focuses on your students a) being able to hear and react on a moment's notice, and b) release the idea of right and wrong. After all, there isn't necessarily a "right or wrong" way to run, stop, or clap.

Instruct the students to stand at one end of the studio. Have three or four of them step forward to form a line (think getting ready to do progressions across the floor). The rest of the students line up behind one of the lead students.

Next, instruct the lead students to follow your vocal instructions.

- When you say the word "run," they are to start running toward the other side of the studio.
- When you say "stop," they are to stop.
- If, and when, you say "Change," they are to switch the position of their feet.
  - For example, if a student were running, and you yelled "stop," and she/he/they stopped with their right foot in front and their left foot behind, when you yell "Change," she/he/they would then switch their right foot back and their left foot front.
  - If you were to yell "Change-Change," then the student would change their foot placement twice – essentially ending their foot placement in the same location when they had first stopped.

Continue the exercise by instructing dancers from the first line (now in the middle of the room) to run again when you yell, "Run." The next line of students will also begin when you yell "Run."

You should continue this exercise until each line of students has made it across the room. Once all students have completed the exercise, have them repeat the exercise, but this time heading back in the opposite direction.

After several times of doing this (i.e. running back and forth across the room – following your commands to "run," "stop," and "change"), you may add "Clap" as an additional task/vocal instruction. You will yell "Clap" only after yelling "Stop." This will ensure your students don't trip and/or stumble.

Rule #1 – There Is No Right or Wrong

- When you yell "Clap," the students will perform a change of the feet, while simultaneously clapping their hands above their heads.
- Be sure to mention that their arms should be straight, so as to keep the hands as far above the head as possible.

The final action/instruction is "Clap-Clap." Once again, this will only be called after yelling "Stop."

- When "Clap-Clap" is yelled, the students will perform a "Change-Change" action with their feet, while clapping twice above their head.
- However, unlike the basic "Change-Change" instruction where students face the same direction they were running while changing their feet, when "Clap-Clap" is called out, they will rotate 180 degrees on the first foot change/clap and continue rotating an additional 180 degrees (ending up facing the same direction they were originally running) on the second foot change/clap.

As you continue to use this exercise from class to class, be sure to:

- Change up your timing. Try to avoid calling out the instructions in a manner that establishes a pattern, predictable time, or order. The point is for the students to hear and react in the moment.
- Avoid rushing to "Change-Change" too quickly. A danger for us teachers is to want to get to the end or hardest part of any exercise too quickly. The first three instructions ("Run," "Stop," and "Change") should be used multiple times over multiple classes before you begin to introduce the more advanced sections of this exercise.
- Remind students that laughter is okay, as long as it doesn't impede their ability to execute the requests of the exercise.

As your students begin to master this exercise, you can complicate it by:

a. Having them run backward.
b. Having them run sideways.
c. Combine running forward and backward in the same pass across the floor.
d. Adapting the word "Change" from an action of changing the feet, to an action of changing height, shape, or facing.

Exercise #3: Across the Floor No Two Ways the Same

This exercise was also introduced to me by the same undergraduate professor (Professor Steven Iannacone), and it remains one of my favorite and consistent exercises I use to teach dance improvisation.

I personally feel that this exercise alone is one of the keys to opening up a student's mind to both dance improvisation and creative movement generation. Like the walking exercise in Chapter 1, this exercise can be used throughout the entire curriculum and can be adapted/adjusted to meet the growing needs of varying levels and ages. For now, we will begin with the simplest form of this exercise.

Like exercise #2, instruct the students to stand at one end of the studio. Have three to four of them step forward to form a line. Have the remaining students line up behind one of the lead students.

Instruct the first line of students that they are to "hop" (two feet to two feet) across the floor to the other side of the room. Every time they land, they are to take a different shape. Your students may ask for clarification (What do you mean by a shape? What kind of shape? Is it a shape with my arms, or my whole body?).

- Resist giving your students clarity, as this is part of the training (remember – Do First, Ask Second). In asking you for clarity, they are really asking "which way is the right way of doing this, and which way is the wrong way of doing this?" Do not give them the clarity (i.e. binary answer) they seek.
- The only rule for this first part of the exercise is that each shape MUST be different from all previous shapes made while hopping across the floor. To add a little fun to this exercise, have the next line of students wait until the first line is half way across the floor. If the second line of students see a student from the first line repeat a shape, they may call out "repeat" and ask the student who repeated a shape to go back to the start and begin again.
- Remind your students that the point of this exercise is to begin exploring new movement and shapes in a manner that is fun. Therefore, when a student says "repeat," it should be said in a helping/amusing manner, rather than judgmental/corrective.
- Once the first line of students is half way across the floor, the second line can begin: which makes the third line of students the observers looking for repeated shapes. When the last line of students is left on the floor, the first

Rule #1 – There Is No Right or Wrong

line of students, who by now have finished, will observe to watch for any repeated shapes.

As your students become more comfortable with this exercise, you can add additional instruction (such as "make round shapes only," or "make low shapes only") to add difficulty and variety. Remember, we are working on expanding their movement vocabulary, as well as forcing them to think creatively in the moment.

After several classes of performing this exercise, you may now move on from making shapes to simply moving across the floor.

- When moving, the student will no longer "hop" in order to travel but will now simply travel through space.
- In order to maintain the improvisational aspect of this exercise, instruct your students to now "move from one side of the room to the other, without repeating the same steps or way of moving." In other words, students must now begin to think about how to move through space without repeating the same way of moving each time.
- For example, if a student were to jeté, they wouldn't be permitted to jeté again as they travel across the floor. If they did, they would be called back to start over.
- You will undoubtedly notice that some, if not all, of your students will start by using familiar dance steps. This is okay for now, but as you continue the exercise, be sure to challenge your students. You can accomplish this by introducing the limitation that no traditional dance steps can be used. This will then force the students to think outside of their "Right and Wrong" dance paradigm, and therefore, forces them to explore new ways of moving.

Finally, as your students practice this exercise over several weeks (or months) of classes, continue to add new challenges with such limitations as:

a. No recognizable dance steps allowed.
b. No cartwheels, back walk-overs, or other acrobatic moves are allowed.
c. Decrease the amount of time they have to travel across the floor. At first, give them all the time they need.
d. Require them to leap only or perhaps keep one hand and one foot attached to the floor at all times.

e. Introduce levels (more about this in Chapter 5).

One Final Thought

You may be asking yourself, "Am I not introducing right and wrong by adding limitations to this exercise?" You may also be asking, "Am I not creating right and wrong by having students call their peers back to the beginning if they repeat a shape/movement?" The simple answer is, yes. However, unlike my tendu example (either it is or it isn't), by adding limitations (I call them "constraints") and accountability to this exercise, you are actually increasing the possibility for discovery, as opposed to limiting the acceptable ways of moving (i.e. perform a tendu only this way).

Limitations and accountability in this case are meant to expand the possibilities of movement, rather than limit them.

Citations

1 Rohr, Richard. *The Universal Christ* (Convergent Books, 2021) - Copyright © 2018 by CAC. Used by permission of CAC. All rights reserved worldwide.
2 Iannacone, Steven. Professor Emeritus, Hope College. 1990–2018.

Notes

Rule #2 – Follow Your Impulse

Introduction

As mentioned in Chapter 3, I tend to teach and work on the first two rules of improvisation simultaneously. Not only are these two rules intrinsically linked in the very nature by which they are subverted by society and culture, but they form a symbiotic relationship during the discovery of each (i.e. to gain progress in one, ultimately means to gain progress in the other). While we need not revisit all of the ways in which culture, society, education, and some forms of dance training have removed young dancers' ability to be spontaneously creative, it is worth taking a few moments to discuss how personal and artistic impulses are affected by these forces.

Context

Some readers of this book may remember a time when recess was, in fact, recess. More than just a time to walk around with friends and gossip while looking at our smartphones, recess was a place where exploration, discovery, and risk-taking could occur. As a child in elementary and middle school, my recess yard had swings, jungle gyms, monkey bars, teeter totters, and a host of other contraptions meant for exploration, play, physical exertion, and, yes, thrill-seeking. These many objects not only built strength and stamina by demanding physical interaction, but they also built an awareness of one's body, physics, and, ultimately, gravity. At the risk of sounding nostalgic (and like my grandfather), I would argue that the playgrounds of today have sacrificed the benefits of physical and cognitive development for safety and cost savings.

The substitution of play equipment with open spaces for today's playgrounds is merely a reflection of the great cultural movement toward safety at all costs.

DOI: 10.4324/9781003387084-5

Rule #2 – Follow Your Impulse

Yes, children, including myself, did injure themselves on these apparatuses, but we also learned much about our bodies. We learned how to move differently, think differently, and solve physical challenges by following our impulse to play. Now that these physical impulses have been removed and replaced with technology, it would seem that children are being forced at even earlier ages to conform to modern society's demands of adulthood.

The name Ido Portal might not mean much to many readers of this book, but it should. Ido Portal was/is an exercise sensation (or dare I say guru) in the mid-2000s. His general premise for health and wellbeing was to educate people on how to reclaim their fullest body mobility through a practice (think curriculum) of basic and fundamental human movement exercises. In other words, his goal was to remove the need for gyms, CrossFit clubs, and all forms of modern exercise and equipment. He preached a message of basics, child-like play, and alternative (some call it holistic) movement practices. In one of his most famous interview and teaching moments discussing parents' frustrations with children playing in the household, Portal expressed irritation that parents yell at their children to stop playing inside simply because it will dirty the walls of the house.

In this interview, Portal was speaking to the practice of parents (myself included) yelling at their children to "stop climbing up the walls." Portal expressed that it was this sort of cultural demand to conform and subdue physical impulses that has led to modern society's overall reduction of basic human mobility and physical wellbeing seen in many American adults. In other words, by demanding that our children stop following their impulses to physically explore the world, try, fail, and play, we have created a new society where adult physical injuries are more prevalent, physical and mental health are on the decline, and the multi-billion-dollar industry of fitness has become the solution to a problem we created.

To use my analogy from a previous chapter, how many parents (including me) can think back to when our children were infants. All we wanted our children to do was roll over. And then, after this was accomplished, we wanted them to crawl. We took videos, pictures, and formed memories of when they actually began to crawl. However, this wasn't good enough for us. Following crawling, we then began to encourage our children to walk….and their first steps were magical. Though, yet again, we weren't satisfied with them existing in a world where they could both crawl and walk, we wanted them to walk only – and walk they did!

By finally walking, our children had achieved the first step on the long journey to becoming an adult. Yet, if we are honest with ourselves, how many times have each of us (again, myself included) found ourselves wishing we had the energy, mobility, and physical aptitude of children? The truth is, in pushing our children through the various stages of mobility as quickly as possible, we removed their physical ability to adapt, maneuver, and develop their full physicality. The question we should ask ourselves is, "At what cost?" Yes, they can now function as a part of normal society, but how many of us as adults now have a hard time keeping up with young children as they play? How many of us wish we had even 5% of the energy, flexibility, and mobility of a child? And, how many of us find ourselves daydreaming about escaping our normal lives and experiencing something different, unusual, and extraordinary? If you are like me, it is quite often.

Is it any wonder then why we are drawn to people who seem to buck the system? We celebrate, if not idolize, the rebel, the against-the-grainer, and the people in our society who seem to live a life outside the boundaries of the 9 to 5 job. As we age, we realize the deal we made as children (unbeknownst to us) to give up our exploration, creativity, and autonomy, in order to enter civilized society, was perhaps a deal where we were not the actual beneficiaries.

To drive this point home, much of performance-focused dance training in the United States has followed this same pattern. If a dancer is lucky, she/he/they at some point participated in a creative dance for children class, or a Mommy and Me class. However, notice that these classes are reserved solely for children. Once a dancer is of the "appropriate age," they then graduate from these exploratory classes to "real dance technique." It is from here they spend their days, and most evening, learning that their bodies must change, their impulses are wrong, and their potential and progress toward a professional career is determined by conformity and traditionalism. The sole purpose of this type of training is to remove all forms of child-like wonder, imagination, and physical exploration. In other words, we want machines, not creative beings.

Please understand that I am by no means diminishing traditional performance-focused dance training, classroom etiquette, or professional decorum. Rather, I am simply explaining the very real and true fact that little (if any) of our students' daily training focuses on continually flexing and working their creative, exploratory, and choice-making muscles. Is it any wonder that our students stare blank-faced at us when we say things like, "It was good, but where is your passion," or "What do you think could happen at this moment in the piece?" So, little of our students' training has been dedicated on how to follow their impulses and express their own personal freedoms. On the contrary, through endless hours of historic repetitive exercises, we run the risk of handing our students movement forms ripe with submission, orthodoxy, and likeness.

Considerations

Acknowledging that personal and creative impulse is a thing long-lost to our childhood, the question is, how do we get it back?

First, we must understand that not only have we been pushed into a world of binary thinking, but second, and equally devious, is that we have lost all contact and control of our impulses. What, you may ask, is an impulse? According to Merriam-Webster's dictionary, impulses are "a sudden spontaneous inclination or incitement to some usually unpremeditated action (1a)", or "a propensity or natural tendency usually other than rational (1b)."[1]

Did you catch the second option for this definition (i.e. *usually other than rational*)? There is it again, a negative connotation toward impulses that must be squashed due to its irrationality. Alas, let us simply state for this chapter, and this book, that impulses are based in the first portion of this definition – "sudden, spontaneous, and unpremeditated."

Understanding acknowledgment is just the first step, we must now investigate the purpose and reason for impulses. I break impulses into two separate categories: **Biological** and **Non-Biological.**

- **Biological** impulses are those items by which the body reacts either without your conscious knowledge (i.e. breathing, heartbeat, metabolism, etc.), or actions taken by you/your body in response to an impulse that arises due to naturally occurring event (i.e. hunger, using the restroom, sleeping, etc.).
    - To categorize these items, biological impulses that are acted upon without consciousness are called *Involuntary Biological Impulses*, and impulses that are consciously acted upon due to nature/evolution are called *Voluntary Biological Impulses*. This same methodology applies to *Non-Biological Impulses*.
- **Non-Biological** impulses are the focus of this chapter. Like *Biological Impulses, Non-Biological Impulses* exist in two subcategories: External and Internal.
    - *External Non-Biological Impulses* are those actions taken by the body where external forces/ideas/inspirations are the impetus for movement.
    - Internal *Non-Biological Impulses* are those actions taken by the body where inner forces (i.e. your imagination) are the impetus for movement.

Figure 4.1 demonstrates these various categories and subcategories.

Rule #2 – Follow Your Impulse

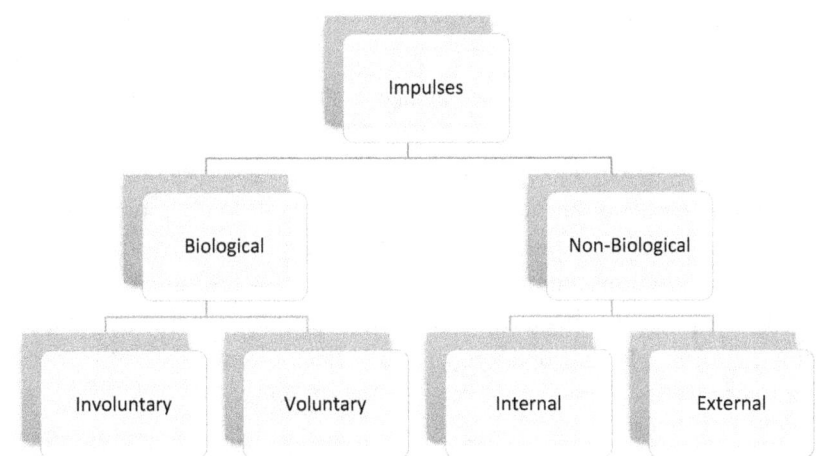

Figure 4.1 Impulse Category Chart

When investigating *Non-Biological External* and *Internal Impulses*, it can be confusing to parcel these two items out. After all, if an external force causes inspiration in me to move, doesn't that impulse first have to flow through my mind? The answer is yes. However, the difference is this: *External Non-Biological Impulses* are chiefly found through external stimuli (think of your five senses), whereas *Internal Non-Biological Impulses* are those inspirations that rise up within you and are not dependent on an external stimulus. For example, have you ever merely been walking down the street and suddenly a creative idea pops in your mind? Perhaps it is a dance step, a picture of a shape, a feeling, or even a series of choreographic movements that has nothing to do with a dance piece you are currently working on. If so, congratulations! You have experienced an *Internal Non-Biological Impulse*.

Now that we understand the various types of impulses, the greater question now is, "How do we actually train our dancers to experience and follow impulses?" It is at this point I want to stress that my *10 Rules of Improvisation: Plus 1* is a continuum, or better yet, a matrix. When exploring any given rule, an improviser should always keep all other rules in mind. Therefore, yes, we want our students to be able to tap into and act on their impulses but not in a manner that is unsafe (i.e. *There is No Right or Wrong, but Sometimes There is a Better Choice*).

The following exercises are actually theater games I learned in my acting training. I enjoy these games for two reasons:

1. Similar to our juggling exercise and *Run, Stop, Change*, these games are not based in dance and therefore they place all participants on the same level.

2. The games also require dance students to speak: something they are all terrified to do. This vocal discomfort is intentional, as it is a way to start breaking the social, cultural, and dance baggage discussed earlier in this chapter.

All three of the following exercises force students to confront both their culturally programmed ideas surrounding impulses, as well forcing them to tap into their *Non-Biological Impulses* (both external and internal). By practicing these exercises multiple times per class, as well as over the course of several weeks or months, dancers will begin to learn to a) let go of societal expectations surrounding appropriate and unappropriated behavior/impulses, and b) begin to find and listen to their own actual *Non-Biological Impulses*.

Try

Exercise #1 – The Machine Game

Start by having the students sit along a wall, leaving the center of the studio open. Next, instruct the students that at any time one, or multiple, of them is permitted to stand up, walk to the center of the space, and execute a repeated action that is accompanied by a noise (i.e. follow their impulse).

- For example; a student may simply stand up, walk to the middle of the room, saw their hand back and forth in the air (as if using a saw), and make a "shhhh – shhhhh" noise with their mouth (mimicking the sound of wood being cut).
- The sound need not imitate an actual sound they hear in their daily lives (eventually it shouldn't), but to aid them in starting, you may allow them to start with familiar sounds/noises.

The action created by the first student, intern, should supply the rest of the students with an *External Non-Biological* stimulus/impulse, where they can then join/add on to the current student's action and noise.

- As more students are added to the group, we have now build a "machine" with many moving parts/actions and many different sounds occurring simultaneously.

Rule #2 – Follow Your Impulse

Once the machine is completely built (i.e. all students are participating), tell the students to stop and sit down.

A singular student will start the next machine following her/his/*their Internal Non-Biological Impulse*, and the other students will add on as a result of the *External Non-Biological Impulse* provided by the newly developing machine.

A few notes to consider:

a. Be sure to have your students repeat this game multiple times, therefore creating multiple machines. As the old saying goes, practice makes perfect.
b. Do not choose a student to start. Force them to sit in silence (if need be) for minutes at a time, until one of them rises and walks to the center. Choosing a student to go first lays the groundwork that it is more important to start than it is to actually discover an impulse. Also, if the instructor becomes uncomfortable with the long periods of silence before a student steps forward, then the students recognize that they simply need to wait long enough and they (the students) won't have to make a choice. This, in turn, removes the whole point of the exercise, which is to listen for and follow a *Non-Biological Internal* impulse.
c. After several times of repeating this game, ask the students if they recognize any similarities between the various machines built. Chances are, they will. Some of these may include:
   a. The noises made tend to reflect real-world noises (i.e. if I am sawing the air with my hand, I may make a sound like a saw cutting wood).
   b. The machine tends to be built in a straight line.
   c. The students tend to remain standing while performing the action and noise (i.e. there is no vertical dynamic to the machine).
   d. The machine will tend to always face "front" (i.e. the audience of students sitting).
   e. The machine noises will tend to fall into a rhythm that mimics a general 4/8-time signature.
   f. The students will tend to use only their arms to make actions.
   g. The machine remains stationary in its original location.
d. All of the above are completely normal since they are parts of the pre-programmed external forces discussed earlier: cultural, social, and dance norms that have been drilled into our students. However, after pointing

Rule #2 – Follow Your Impulse

these items out, now challenge your students to build a machine that goes against these norms.

    a. To begin, rather than have the students sit along a singular wall, have them sit in a giant circle. After all, changing their perspective may assist in helping them break out of their historic norms.[2]

e. After each machine is built, be sure to circle up with the students to debrief and discuss. This allows for two items:

    a. It lays the groundwork for the rest of this book where discussion after exercises is an integral part of the training.

    b. It allows time and space for the students to make discoveries with each other. The more connections and discoveries students can make on their own and with their fellow students, the more their learning will increase and curiosity will develop.

        i. Remember, our goal is to ultimately train dancers who can think, act, analyze, create, perform, and play through their own self-direction. These learning circles are the beginning of this journey.

Exercise #2 – The Object Game

Similar to the machine game, the object game is meant to introduce students to the idea of following their non-biological impulses. However, unlike the machine game, this game is completely motivated by the students' external impulses.

- Have the students sit in a giant circle around the room.
- In the middle of the circle, you will place an object.
- On their own time, students are allowed to walk to the center of the circle and use/play with the object. The caveat, however, is that the students cannot use the object for its originally intended purpose. For example, if you place a chair in the middle of the circle, the students can use the chair for anything other than sitting (i.e. as a chair).

A few notes to consider:

a. Encourage students to use vocalizations to accompany their play. Again, vocalizing is an act many dancers are terrified of, and therefore, it is good practice to continue to work on this item. Additionally, vocalizing breaks them out of their normalized dance training (i.e. be quiet when moving).

b. To assist students, I usually start with a larger object, and one that has as much potential for reinterpretation. A chair is a great object to begin with. From here, I then begin to choose smaller and smaller objects, until the final object being used is a tennis ball, or the center core of a roll of toilet paper roll.

c. It may be helpful to adjust the objects presentation if you feel your students are struggling. For example, after a few minutes, I will tip a chair on its side – or perhaps upside down. As mentioned earlier, a change in one's perspective is necessary in order to increase one's creativity.

d. You yourself may have to demonstrate, both at the beginning and as students get stuck. Students are always afraid of looking silly in front of one another, and therefore, it is up to us as teachers to lead the way in play.

e. Like the machine game, do not be afraid of long moments of silence. Allow the students to sit in the silence, thus reinforcing that you as the instructor won't simply move on because they refuse to participate. After some silence has passed, you can either (a) adjust the object's presentation, or (b) demonstrate an example as a means of spurring the students' imaginations.

f. Before introducing a new object, be sure to take time to discuss. What did the students find hard about the previous object? What did they find easy? Were they nervous to participate? Why? What did they see/learn from the other students who participated? How will they use this knowledge with the next object?

Exercise #3 – The Clapping Exercise

For this exercise, break your students into smaller groups (ideally four to six students in each group). Larger groups can make dancers self-conscious, therefore I tend to prefer smaller groups as a means of easing both anxiety and stage fright.

As always, remind your students that dance improvisation class is a place to feel and be safe, and therefore whatever happens in dance improvisation class, stays in improvisation class. I mention this again only because as we increase the number, level, and difficulty of each exercise, the more students must be vulnerable in order for the exercises to have the greatest impact. *Vulnerability*

Rule #2 – Follow Your Impulse

cannot exist in a world without trust. Be sure to remind your students of this point.

- Have each group sit in their own small circle and ask one person from each group to volunteer to step into and stand the middle of their circle.
- The task is simple: the person in the middle of each group will make a shape with their body each time she/he/they hears a member of their group clap.
- If multiple claps occur simultaneously (let's say three claps), then the person in the middle must do three rapid shapes.
- Allow this exercise to continue for some time before rotating students in the center of each circle.

Once all groups are complete (i.e. each person from each group has been in the center of their circle), gather together as a class to discuss and debrief.
A few notes to consider:

a. Encourage each student who is in the middle of each circle to close his/her/their eyes. Something magical occurs when we close our eyes. All inhibitions seem to fade away, and we become less concerned about those around us.

b. Encourage the seated students in the circles to start off clapping **slowly**. This is not the time for sink-or- swim. Rather, the student in the center should have ample time to hear an individual clap, process it, and react to it by taking a new shape. This process is how students begin to build trust with one another.

c. After all of the circles have completed one round, take time to process and debrief. Ask the following questions as prompts:

   i. What parts of the body did we tend to use most to make shapes? Are there other parts of the body we can make shapes with? What about the whole body?

   ii. Did we tend to stay standing the whole exercise, or did we explore multiple vertical levels? Why or why not?

   iii. Did our shapes tend to be angular or round? Why? What may lead to choosing one over the other?

iv. Did we tend to face the same direction always? Why or why not?

v. Did we ever put our backs or stomachs to the floor? Why or why not?

vi. Did our shapes tend to be large or small? Why or why not?

vii. How can we challenge ourselves next time?

d. Repeat the exercise, but this time allowing more claps to occur at a more rapid rate.

   i. Once a second round is complete, gather the students together again for discussion.

   ii. Based on what you observed during the second round, formulate more questions/prompts to ask your students.

   iii. Remember, you as the instructor must remain present at all times in order to see what is going on and adjust your class/questions as needed.

e. Repeat a third round of this exercise allowing multiple claps to occur simultaneously: thus forcing the student in the center of the circle to react without any time to think. This forces the student in the center to truly act upon their immediate impulse and removes time for them to process/think.

Citations

1 "Impulse" *Merriam-Webster.com*. 2023. https://www.merriam-webster.com/dictionary/impulses?utm_campaign=sd&utm_medium=serp&utm_source=jsonld (6 June 2023).

2 I tell my students all of the time, "your creativity is limited merely by your perspective."

Notes

Rule #3 – Start with What You Know

Introduction

Now that I have spent the last several chapters exposing all of the ways our students' creativity and movement vocabulary has been suppressed by culture, society, and traditional technical training in dance, I want to spend this chapter reminding us that not all parts of our historic, performance-focused dance training are bad. On the contrary, there is much in our students' training that can be drawn upon for the dance improvisation process. Additionally, meeting our students at their comfort level is the key to exposing them to dance improvisation without terrifying them.

Unfortunately, I have seen some dance improvisation teachers tell students to "Forget everything you know," or "Get ready to have your world rocked." Sadly, approaches such as these only scare students away from a technique (again I stress that dance improvisation is a technique) that is meant to further develop both their physical and artistic training. As I tell my students all of the time, "The issue isn't that you have habits, it's that you can't control them; and *a habit that can't be controlled is called an addiction*." The goal of dance improvisation is not to throw the baby out with the bath water but rather to add additional training and versatility to our students.

The purpose of this chapter is to remind us as teachers, and subsequently our students, that what you know isn't wrong; it simply isn't all there is to know.

Context

A major part of dance training is revisiting exercises, concepts, and ideas. After all, how many tendus and plies will a dancer do in her/his/their lifetime? How many contractions, jazz squares, single time-steps, or a host of other physical executions have we all done in our prospective fields of study? The reality is that when creating

DOI: 10.4324/9781003387084-6

Rule #3 – Start with What You Know

most dance classes, we tend to start with what we know. Since we understand the pedagogical reason for this, why should improvisation class be any different?

This portion of the dance improvisation curriculum is meant to serve just this purpose: go back and revisit everything that has been done and learned thus far. Do not rush to the finish line. After all, this is dance/art, there is no finish line. By revisiting exercises and concepts from the previous chapters, you and your students will be amazed to see not only how far you have come but all of the new discoveries made now that things feel more comfortable.

Before we dive into exercises, I feel compelled to speak directly to any teacher who may criticize their students for previous training that relied on "tricks." It is imperative for us as successful dance improvisation teachers to understand that physical prowess is not something to be shunned. After all, tricks (as we like to call them) are nothing more than a small portion of what I call the **Human Movement Buffet.** Yes, tricks are a small portion, and our desire is for our students to expand their movement palette of the buffet, but tricks in and of themselves are not bad.

I stress this only because too many times I have seen teachers criticize, belittle, and bemoan students for starting with what a student knows. If dance improvisation classes are meant to serve as a place to be vulnerable, then no student has ever felt the ability to be vulnerable around an instructor who was condescending. We must always lead by example and therefore use process and patience as our guide.

Lastly, I also want us as teachers to take a moment to stop and reflect on "starting with what we know." Many readers of this book will have been teaching for 20, 30, or perhaps even 40 years. We have an encyclopedia of pedagogical knowledge and experience from which to draw. We know how to create a class, a curriculum, and how to adapt teaching in the moment in order to serve the needs of the students in front of us. We have innumerable examples of repeating exercises so our students get the concept, or walking into a class and realizing that what we prepared was either too advanced or too easy.

All of this is to say that we inherently understand that teaching dance, and teaching in general, is a full contact event. We must be both physically and mentally present at every moment of the class in order to serve our students to the very best of our (and their) ability. Therefore, remember that teaching improvisation is the exact same. You may (or let me simply say, you will) have to repeat exercises. You will have to slow some things down and speed some things up. You will have to pause class and take time to process what has occurred. You will have to add to the exercises in this book, as well adapt them in the moment to accommodate what you see before you. You have the knowledge. Trust that.

After all, good teaching (as a colleague and mentor of mine likes to say) is about leading a class not giving a class.

Now, you may still be asking yourself, "So what is it that Matt is so confident I know?" Well, simply put, you know the structure of a dance class and how to put it together. Unarguably, each dance technique is different and unique, and therefore, content dictates *what* you will teach. But *how* you teach a class, and how that class is structured is fairly standard: warm-up, move, group work. While these three basic classifications may seem crude and elementary, they are, in fact, how most dance classes are taught.

- Warm-ups may look different based on the specific style (ballet = barre, modern = floor, jazz = isolations, tap = ankle and hip work, hip hop = finding your groove, etc.), but the basic premise is the same among all of them: to warm up both the mind and body, while simultaneously working on smaller technical elements (i.e. balance, strength, turning, fluidity, etc.).
- Next, generally comes some form of additional movement, and, again, depending on the style/technique, this may look different. Ballet would include tendus and turns at center, Modern may include across the floor or down the diagonal, and Jazz may include progressions. You get the point. The whole idea behind that the next portion of class is to begin putting all of the bits and pieces in the warm-up section together into motion and locomotion. Make it all work together while moving through space.
- Lastly, we generally wrap up with some form of group work. It may be a combination at the end of class, an adage, petite allegro and grand allegro, a cipher, or any other form of event that causes the students to begin applying everything from class into the practice of performance.

You see, you do know where to begin!

Structuring Your Class

The beauty of approaching dance improvisation as a technique is that it follows this very same class structure. There are games and exercises we play in order to warm up the students' minds and bodies. These games and exercises many times are stationary, or, at the very least, move very little throughout space. Their purpose and meaning is to warm-up and begin working on smaller ideas and elements of dance improvisation. In this section of the class, think of the exercises we have

Rule #3 – Start with What You Know

already explored: juggling, the machine game, and the object game. There are a few additional games we have not discussed (such as drawing your name in space with your boy, making a shape with your body every time the teacher says a color, etc.), but for now, simply recognize that, like any other dance class, we wouldn't ask our students to start flinging themselves through space two minutes into the class. Again, the point of this portion of the class (like all beginning portions of dance classes) is to awaken both the body and mind of the students.

Following singularly focused and generally stationary warm-ups, we would next move onto exercises that cause the students to move more throughout the space. This may include such games as Through Space No Two Ways the Same, the Walking Exercise, and a host of other exercises that cause the students to begin to use more of their bodies in a locomotive manner. We may choose to also direct some of these exercises by increasing their difficulty (see Exercise #1 in this chapter), or we may choose to have students execute these exercises multiple times, asking them to try a new approach each time. All of this with a goal to continue the warming up of the mind and body, while working ever closer to the lesson and group experience for the day's theme.

The third section of the class is the lesson/theme for the day/week. This series of exercises are meant to introduce students to a new concept, while still drawing on the concepts they have worked on thus far. A great ballet teacher once told me, "if you want to create a great ballet class, start from the end and work your way backward; reminding yourself that every exercise along the way should prepare students for the final exercise you have created." I find this suggestion to be extremely helpful not just in ballet classes but in all dance technique classes. After all, a combination at the end of class should be the highlight of everything the students have worked toward. Yes, it is the practice of performance, but what good is that practice if they haven't worked on any of the physical executions up until this point? So it is with dance improvisation.

The lesson/theme of the class/week is the moment to take time in class. In the earlier portions of the curriculum, this may be yet another group exercise (see Exercise #2 in this chapter), or in later portions of the curriculum/year, it may be small, guided improvisations. All this being said, it is here where things should not be rushed, and time should be dedicated for discussion. It is here where students will begin to make discoveries, and you as a teacher can begin to add insight, observations, and guidance (not corrections) into how students can further develop the next time.

The final portion of the class is the group work. In the early stages of the curriculum, this is perhaps where you insert the Machine Game or the Object

Game. In the later portions of the curriculum, this is where we actually begin to execute small and large group improvisations. It is a way to bring the class together and find a collective community among them, while simultaneously dedicating a portion of class to the practice of performance. Again, this portion of the class is completely useless if the practice is not a continuation of what has been worked on thus far. However, your watchful eye is needed even more in this section of the class since dance improvisations conducted by young improvisers tend to venture into territory not yet discussed.

Considerations

Before we dive into the exercises for this chapter, let's take a quick moment to discuss demonstrating. Hopefully, you are starting to see the pattern of this book. While I am generally a fan of instructors demonstrating in dance classes (after all I am sure we can all remember that one time that "ancient" teacher did something that amazed and inspired us to be better), I generally frown upon teachers demonstrating during the actual improvisation portion of class.

When we demonstrate in other dance classes, we are inevitably telling our students "execute in the same manner as me." Because of this training, the moment we demonstrate in an improvisation class our students fall right back into the dualist thinking of right and wrong, which is, again, the opposite of what we want them to do. Therefore, if you are going to demonstrate, be sure to keep it limited and use phrases such as, "You could consider this option," or "One way to address this might be."

Open-ended statements similar to those above allow the students to understand that what you are about to do is not the only way, or even the right way, but simply one of many options. Remember, our goal is to get our students to eat from the entire **Human Movement Buffet** not just the section that we frequent.

Try

Exercise#1 – Revisit Across the Floor No Two Ways the Same

You have already worked with your students on the No Two Ways the Same Exercise, but it is worth repeating. In fact, I find that in the course of a semester or

Rule #3 – Start with What You Know

year, I will use this exercise as a part of my improvisation class more than 60% of the time. The students eventually get to love this exercise, and they discover new things along the way. Additionally, you will begin to notice that each student will start to form new habits (we as humans love our habits), and it is at this time you can start to add what I call *constraints*.

Constraints are nothing more than guidelines that make this exercise more difficult to accomplish. I believe it was Igor Stravinsky who once said, "The more constraints one imposes, the more one frees one's self." In the spirit of this idea, confinements are the very thing your students will need in order to break their new found habits in this exercise.

Here are examples of constraints you may wish to add:

(a) Levels – Take time to discuss the various vertical levels available to students. You can use any number of words or explanations, but generally, I break up levels into three main categories: **Low, Medium, and High**.

   i. Low-level movement is any movement that uses the entire body but restricts it to a vertical plane no higher than 24" off the ground (approximately the height of a person's knee). Think crawling, rolling, summersaults, log rolls, slithering, the worm, etc.

   ii. Medium-level movement is any movement that uses the entire body but restricts it to a vertical plane of between 24" off the ground to 42" off the ground, or approximately a vertical space that exists between the height of a kneecap and the height of a ballet barre. In this space, you can imagine a bear walk, crab crawls, low-level cartwheels, squatting, etc.

   iii. High-level movement is any movement that uses the entire body and exists in vertical plane between 42" and the stratosphere. This area would include full-size cartwheels, jumps, leaps, hops, grande jetes, and, sarcastically speaking, levitation.

   By confining your students to a singular vertical level, or perhaps two conjoining levels (i.e. low and medium level only, or medium and high level only), you will force them to work in spaces that are both unfamiliar and uncomfortable, thus expanding their movement vocabulary while simultaneously breaking them of their new found habits.

(b) Body Parts – Another way to create constraints for your students in this exercise is by limiting them to using only specific body parts, ruling out the use of certain body parts, or limiting the number of contact points that they can have with the ground.

      i. You will probably have noticed by this point in the curriculum that when executing this specific exercise, students will resort to moving through space and making shapes in a manner that is most comfortable to them. I usually see this through the execution of such items as grand jetes, cartwheels, and making shapes with their arms.

     ii. Confining your students to using only specific body parts (or in the case of their arms, not allowing them to use their arms) forces them out of these pre-established patterns.

    iii. Additionally, by limiting the number of contact points they may have with the ground (i.e. you may only have three contact points, or you may only have two contact points), you again force your students to explore new and interesting ways of locomotion through space.

(c) Texture – A rather fun and less physically demanding constraint you can apply to this e.xercise is that of texture. Using texture imagery is a great way to encourage your students to move in a manner different from their preferred signature style.

      i. You can use such instruction as "move through the space, no two ways the same, but only in a fluid manner," or "move through the space, no two ways the same, but in an angular manner."

     ii. These types of constraints are great because they also force the students to reach into their creativity by giving them a task that they must first interpret with their mind and then execute, rather than the mere physical-based constraints mentioned earlier.

    iii. Be creative and have some fun with texture. Once students get used to singular texture words (rigid, soft, round, square, etc.), begin to explore suggested confinements that tap even further into their creativity. Ask them to move through the space, no two ways the same, but like an elephant; or, move through space, no two ways the same, but under immense gravity (or no gravity at all). Move through space, no two ways the same, like the color blue – or fuchsia.

(d) Time – Time is another great constraint to use. At first, allow your students all of the time they need in order to simply accomplish the task (as mentioned in Chapter 3). Too many times, I have seen teachers push their students to move too quickly, which inevitably frustrates both the students and the teacher. Remember, you wouldn't ask a beginning ballet student to do an advanced step, so don't force a beginning dance improvisation student to move too quickly.

Rule #3 – Start with What You Know

    i. Once your students are comfortable with this exercise (you can tell because they will be having fun and moving with ease), you can now adjust how much time they have to accomplish the task.

    ii. First, start by giving them 30 seconds to accomplish this exercise. They will all freak out and say "That's impossible!" Remind them that they once thought this exercise alone was impossible, and therefore, you have complete confidence in them to be able to accomplish this new constraint.

    iii. After several times of attempting this exercise with only 30 seconds available, turn up the heat (as it were) by giving them now only 20 seconds.

    iv. Following this, you can continue to decrease the time by 5 or 10 second intervals.

    v. Repeat the sequence (i.e. lather, rinse, repeat).

Once the students feel comfortable with, say, 10 seconds to accomplish the task, now tip the scales in the other extreme.

    i. Go back to 30 seconds for cross the floor but remind the students that they must use ALL 30 seconds. After they have adjusted back to what feels like eternity to them, begin to add time.

    ii. Start by upping the time to 45 seconds: again reminding them that they must use ALL 45 seconds, or they will have to go back to the beginning.

    iii. Continue this progression until you have reached a time length that forces them to move ever continually slower. For example, I would say 2 minutes is certainly not out of the question. In fact, one of my improvisation teachers once used this exercise for the entire class and informed us we had to use the entire class time (90 minutes) to cross the space of the room. While this at the time felt excruciating (and I certainly wouldn't recommend this for younger students), the idea of learning to be intentional about your movement is something worth exploring with today's students. You will see an expanded version of this exercise in Chapter 11.

(e) Combine Two or More Constraints – This constraint speaks for itself. After many classes, maybe even weeks, of exploring singular confinements, you can begin to combine two of these confinements. Again, always remember that the purpose of these constraints is to encourage our students to expand their movement vocabulary and not to frustrate them with overly difficult tasks.

Exercise #2 – Revisit the Clapping Game

Now that your students are comfortable with the clapping game, you can begin to add constraints in this exercise as well. Aside from using all of the constraints mentioned in Exercise #1 of this chapter, you can create your own. As mentioned before, start with physical constrains (i.e. shapes, limbs, etc.) at first but then create constraints that force students to tap into their imagination. Remember, have *serious fun*.

Exercise #3 – Mirror Exercise

Though this exercise is new for this curriculum, its origins reach back to our earliest days of existing on this planet. Babies and children learn and grow in their developmental years through mirroring and repetition. Therefore, we are in essence returning "back to the beginning" for this exercise.

- Have your students pair up. A simple way to ensure the same students don't always partner up is to have them first walk around the room in a random pattern. At any moment, you can instruct them to "stop." Next, tell them to reach their right (or left) hand in the air. Next, grab the hand of a person closest to them and, viola, they have their partner.
- Once partnered up, have each pair pick a Person A and a Person B. As the instructor, begin to count down out loud from 5 to 0. This ensures efficiency and forces the students to make a choice and go with it. This reinforces following impulses.
- Next, have Person A and Person B face one another. Person A will be the leader, and Person B be the follower. Instruct Person A to move slowly, and only use their hands and arms only at first. The point of this exercise is for Person A and Person B to be so in sync with one another that you as the instructor cannot tell who is leading and who is following. After several minutes, instruct them to switch who is leading and who is following.

Some additional notes to consider:

a. You will notice that at first there will be some laughter and giggles. This is completely normal and common. However, remind the students that as a part of the process we are always building, or losing, trust with the people we share

Rule #3 – Start with What You Know

the space with. Giggling is a form of release when something is uncomfortable. Rather than criticize the students for this, take a moment after the first round of mirroring (Person A leading and then Person B leading) to discuss this concept. Pose questions such as, "Why are we giggling?" or, "What makes this exercise uncomfortable?" The answers will vary from student to student and class to class, but they will also be informative for you as the instructor on how to proceed. Once you have taken time to discuss this first round, repeat a second round, reminding them to move slowly and limit the giggling.

b. Continually remind your students to **SLOW DOWN**. We live in a fast-paced world, where anything other than continual and rapid movement feels unproductive, and therefore, we feel the need to move quickly. We will discuss this more in Chapter 10. Remind the students that their job as the leader is to take care of their partner (the follower), and therefore, the slower they move, the easier it is for their partner to follow them.

c. If your students are struggling, also consider instructing them to move smaller. Contrary to a popular idea in America, bigger is not always better. Again, it is harder to following someone who is moving too big. Plus, moving smaller will force your students to learn and adapt to new textures and ways of moving, thus expanding their **Human Movement Buffet**.

d. After each round (Person A leading and then Person B), take time for discussion. I cannot express enough that discoveries via discussion are just as important in this process as are the exercises themselves.

e. Feel free to have the students change partners after several rounds. Changing partners again introduces your students to new movers and ways of moving, as well as forming bonds across the class.

f. Encourage your students to look directly into one another's eyes. This will again manifest some giggling, but it is an extremely important part of this process. It accomplished two items:

   i. It forces our students to look someone else in the eyes. Too much of our society today is spent looking at others through the lens of television, our phones, and filters used in our online accounts. Something magical occurs when we look at another human directly in the eyes for a long period of time. Additionally, much of society has taught us that looking into someone's eyes has some sort of physical or sexual connotation. Forcing your students to look into each other's eyes begins to break down these preconceived notions. It is also great groundwork in preparation for ideas and exercise discussed in Chapter 7.

  ii. By looking into the eyes of their partner, the students are no longer able to directly look at the appendage they are trying to mirror. Looking straight forward allows the students to see the whole of their partner and thus tap into their own peripheral vision. This skill will become increasingly important as they advance in this book's curriculum.

g. After several classes, begin to instruct your students to change between Person A leading and Person B leading as the exercise is occurring. At first, you will have to verbally tell them ("Person B now leads" or "Back to Person A"), but eventually, the goal is for the students to fluidly flow between Person A and Person B leading without any direct verbal communication from you as the instructor and without any verbal or physical communication between them. Again, the whole idea of this exercise is for each pair of students to be perfectly in sync with one another. They will change between who is leading and who is following, without an outside person being able to tell who is leading and who is following.

h. The greater purpose of this exercise (in addition to those items already mentioned) is to practice, and eventually master, working and moving in the moment. By tapping into the now of the exercise, while focusing all energy on the other person, each student is beginning to learn the technical skill of the cycle of improvisation discussed in Chapter 1.

i. After several classes, students can begin to also explore movement outside of just their hands and arms. Encourage them to **slowly** incorporate other body parts, different vertical levels, as well as trying to make the pairing move through space, all the while remembering to pause between each cycle to discuss new ideas and findings.

Notes

Rule #4 – When in Doubt, Go Back to the Beginning

Introduction

By this point in your students' journey, they will have become comfortable with the uncomfortable, learned how to separate and understand their various impulses, and are beginning to enjoy, if not anticipate, the idea of improvisation as an integral part of dance training. It is exactly at this point where we need to now slow the process down and revisit a few items. Similar to raising pre-teens, your students are at that point where they know enough to be somewhat independent but not enough to function safely in a fully developed dance improvisation. Also like pre-teens, they will groan and fuss over the idea that they don't actually know it all (image that). It is exactly for this reason that we must now revisit all of the lessons from the previous chapters.

Context

To begin with, if you haven't begun to complicate the warm-ups from previous chapters, now is the time to do it. This is also the time for you as a teacher to introduce and try your own exercises that you have developed based on the first three rules. Lastly, this is also the time to introduce alternative exercises that you may have learned in workshops or in additional books on this subject. All these being said, the pre-teen years of this curriculum are perhaps the most critical part. If we are successful in this stage, then it is here where we will set our students up for a journey of self-discovery, awareness, and eager playfulness. However, if we are unsuccessful at this point, then students will leave this process

DOI: 10.4324/9781003387084-7

Rule #4 – When in Doubt, Go Back to the Beginning

thinking improvisation is simply something fun to do as a distraction/break from "real technique." The stakes are high.

I first recommend revisiting the juggling exercise. By this point, you may have removed this exercise from the students' daily warmup. This is completely understandable since there are only so many minutes in a class, only so many classes in a week, and only so many exercises one can accomplish, especially if you need (and you will need) to repeat exercises multiple times in the same class period. However, the juggling exercise (as I mentioned earlier) is the personification of improvisation.

- There is a basic structure. Adaptation is mandatory.
- It follows the cycle of improvisation. It demonstrates this rule clearly.
- When a student drops a juggling item during this exercise, she/he/they must quite literally return to the beginning, thus restarting the process of execution and learning for the student.

Therefore, return to the juggling exercise as an embodiment of this rule and chapter.

If you haven't complicated the juggling exercise yet for the students, now is the time. By now, they should be able to juggle while walking forward around the room. If they are not capable of this yet, then this is where you start. If they are capable of walking forward while juggling, now have them walk backward, or perhaps –

- Walk sideways, around the room.
- Close one eye, which limits their proprioception.
- If they were using silk scarves, now is the appropriate time to have them switch to hacky sacks.
- If they were using hacky sacks, have them now use tennis balls.
- For a real challenge, have them use one of each (i.e. a silk scarf, a hacky sack, and a tennis ball).

Lastly, if you see that your students' progress in juggling has waned, ask them why this has occurred. You will most likely discover that they stopped practicing once the exercise was removed from the class structure. This behavior is normal not just for juggling but for all things related to dance. However, ask your students these two simple questions:

Rule #4 – When in Doubt, Go Back to the Beginning

(1) Do you (the students) use class as your practice time, or do you practice outside of class in order to get better in class?

(2) If you do practice outside of class, what do you practice and why?

You will probably not be surprised to hear the answer to question #1 that our students tend not to practice outside of class, or maybe I am alone in experiencing this. However, you may be surprised at the answers you receive regarding question #2. The answers your students give to question #2, more so than question #1, will reveal to you as a teacher what messages you and/or your dance studio are sending to your students regarding the hierarchy of importance. Simply put, your students' answers will let you know what you have told them (directly or indirectly) is important to practice.

Why does this matter? For starters, if we know that our students will only be practicing (if at all) what we have deemed as important, then inherently everything else is deemed unimportant and therefore neglected from practice. This goes back to our discussion on binary thinking, and our students' inherent desire to place items into boxes of right and wrong, good and bad, important and unimportant. Therefore, if technical steps are deemed important, then anything that "distracts" from this is thrown to the wind, including the juggling exercise. Perhaps we as teachers can use this rule and chapter to start from **THE** beginning as a means of reexamining how we speak about dance. Simply put, our students should be practicing their juggling just as much as their turns.

Another great series of exercises to return to are the walking exercises from Chapter 1. Yes, you can certainly repeat these exercises as you instructed prior, but I would recommend now allowing your students to blend the exercises. Allow them to transition seamlessly between walking, jogging, bear crawl, crab crawl, etc. This will not only allow them some autonomy in their newly discovered confidence, but it will also warm them up quite quickly since moving between vertical levels is difficult and physically demanding. Additionally, you could have the students walk around with one eye closed the whole time, or you can challenge them more by placing vertical limitations on them as they move throughout the space.

Considerations

As a final note, this chapter and rule serve not only as a means of revisiting lessons once thought mastered, but it also serves as a transition period (back to our pre-teen analogy) into more complicated and multifaceted approaches to improvisation. Until this point, your students have been working mainly in a self-contained and self-focused manner. This was necessary in order for each of them to discover their own fears and trepidations surrounding dance improvisation, address their own movement biases, as well as tap into and discover their own personal impulses. However, at some point, they must enter the world of dance improvisation that contains multiple individuals and learn how to work as a community through a system of adaptation and compromise.

As a means of developing the skills for this next step in their journey, the following exercises lean both on previous exercises from this book, as well as assisting students with dipping their toes into a shared improvisational experience. As always, take it **SLOWLY** (have I made my point yet). There is a reason early middle school looks like high school but has some of the same structures as elementary school. We want to expose students to large changes in a safe and slow manner; otherwise, we risk the chance of losing their progress and interest.

Try

Exercise #1: Tapping into Your Proprioception

Returning to the very first exercise your students learned, you will now instruct them to walk around the room with their eyes completely closed. However, like all things in this book, you will not merely throw them into this exercise.

- Frist, have them all walk around the room like before, allowing them to pause when they desire, and begin walking again when they desire. Be sure not to mention that you will be doing something different today, as this statement can add anxiety before the exercise even begins.
- Consider my recommendation from this chapter. Start first with having your students walk around with one eye closed. This will reduce their peripheral vision while also serving as a great transitioning version of this exercise.
- After the students have progressed through the walking exercise (i.e. walk, fast walk, jog, run, jog, fast walk, walk), have all of them stop in space.
- Now, instruct them to close their eyes and simply listen to their heartbeats, the breathing of their classmates, and any and all other noises they may hear.

Rule #4 – When in Doubt, Go Back to the Beginning

- Now, with the students' eyes still closed, you, the instructor, will inform them that you will tap some of them on the shoulder. Remind them to keep their eyes closed even if you tap them on the shoulder.
- Once you have tapped half of the students' shoulders, you will now instruct the students whose shoulders were tapped to open their eyes and SLOWLY begin walking around the room.
- Be sure to keep an eye out for students who want to "mess" with their fellow classmates (i.e. walk extremely close to them, blow on their faces, poke them, etc.) You will need to stop this behavior immediately if it occurs and remind the class that creativity cannot exist in a world without trust, and the burden of trust falls on those walking around with their eyes open.
- The students who are walking should merely walk through space and avoid any contact with the students standing still.

Meanwhile, the students who are standing stationary with their eyes closed should be instructed to listen and feel for where their fellow students are in space. After the students with their eyes open have walked around for a while, instruct them to find a place to stop and close their eyes.

Repeat the exercise, but reverse the roles of the students.

Once the students have switched roles several times, circle the class up to debrief. Ask your students the following questions:

- What did you experience as someone standing still with their eyes closed?
- What fears (if any) arose in you?
- What did you experience as someone walking around with their eyes open?
- What thoughts (if any) arose in you?
- When your eyes were closed, were you able to guess if someone was close to you? How? What items did you experience that allowed you to discover their proximity?
- Other than sound, what other items did you experience with your eyes closed? (i.e. shadow, light/darkness, heat, electrical energy, etc.)

The purpose of this exercise is to begin developing your students' proprioception: the body's ability to sense movement, action, location, and facing without the use of eyesight. This skill will become increasingly important as improvisations are complicated and more individuals are added. Contrary to what our moms told us (or maybe it was just my mom), we do not have eyes in the back of our heads. Therefore, the ability to be able to identify proximity of others without our eyes is a skill that will need to be learned and trained.

Once you have debriefed, repeat the exercise again. This time, remind the students to start tapping into alternative senses other than sight that will allow them to experience movement in the environment.

Exercise #2: Walking Around the Room with Both Eyes Closed

After your students have spent several classes learning about and building their proprioception, it is now time to advance their learning. Begin this exercise exactly the same way you began exercise #1 in this chapter. This time, however, inform your students that once they have been tapped on the shoulder, they will now begin to walk through the space with their eyes closed.

In other words, everyone will keep their eyes closed at all times; whether they are stationary or walking.

A few items to remind your students of before and during this exercise:

- Walk <u>slowly</u>!!!!!
- Focus less on where you are going and focus more on sensing your way through space.
- Let go of the idea of knowing where you are in the room. Rather, focus merely on those items/people who may be proximal to you.
- If you feel like you are getting close to someone or something, slow down even more and approach them/it with calmness and sensitivity.
- Do not place hands out in front of you. Fingers are pointy objects, and they can either hurt someone or be hurt easily.
- As a substitute for your fingers, feel with the sides of your arms. However, the arms (ideally) should remain by the sides of the body.
- If you bump into someone, don't apologize and don't overreact. Tightening your muscles/body up increases the chance for injury. Rather, soften even more as you slowly stop.

- If you become disoriented, simply stop for a moment to allow your mind and body to catch up to one another.
- Take care of your fellow students who are stationary. They don't want to be bumped into any more than you want to bump into them.

After the students who are walking with their eyes closed have walked around for a while, instruct them to find a place to stop.

Repeat the exercise but reverse the roles of the students.

Once the students have switched roles several times, circle the class up to debrief. Ask your students the following questions:

- What now did you experience while standing still with your eyes closed?
- What now did you experience walking around with your eyes closed?
- What fears arose in you while standing still or walking? Why do you think this is?
- Where you able to tap into your proprioception even more now that the stakes were higher? Why or Why not?
- What can we learn from this exercise: both for dance improvisation and in other forms of dance?

Repeat this exercise several more times and be sure to repeat it over the course of several more classes.

Eventually, you will know your students have achieved a sense of proficiency when they no longer maneuver the space with trepidation and rigid bodies. There will be an ease with which they walk around with their eyes closed, and few to no collisions should occur.

Exercise #3: Group Mirroring

This is a continuation of the mirroring exercise from Chapter 5. However, rather than the exercise occurring between two individuals, it will not occur between a minimum of three people and up to five people.

To begin, break your students into small groups consisting of three, four, or five dancers per group. The number of students assigned to each group will be determined by the total number of students present. If, for example, you have a

Rule #4 – When in Doubt, Go Back to the Beginning

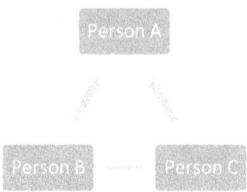

Figure 6.1 Triangle Formation for Group Mirroring Exercise

class of 12 students, you can either break them up into four groups containing three dancers, or three groups containing four dancers. In the ideal situation, you will start with more groups containing three dancers each, and eventually, grow the number of dancers in each group as the students become more comfortable with the exercise.

For a group of three dancers, have them stand in a triangle shape. Appoint a Person A, Person B, and Person C. Person A will be the top of the triangle, and Persons B and C will be the bottom of the triangle. Person A should face away from B and C, and Persons B and C should be facing Person A so as to be staring at Person A's back (Figure 6.1).

Now, instruct Person A to slowly begin moving, while Persons B and C mirror Person A from behind. As they continue to move, if Person A no longer desires to lead, she/he/they can begin to turn to either their right or left; thus bringing Person B or C into their view. Depending on which way they turn, Person A can hand off leadership to Person B or C, who would now take over; thus making them the new top of the triangle.

The exercise continues allowing each person to pass the leadership onto another member of the triangle simply by turning their body to the right or left.

After the various groups have participated in the exercise for some time (ensuring every student has had a chance to be a leader of their group), instruct them to finish and circle up for discussion. Pose these questions to your students during discussion:

* Do you enjoy leading or following? Why?
* Did you as individuals or as a group find yourself settling into a predictable pattern? Why do you think this is?
* As a follower, did you find some of the movements chosen by the leader difficult? Why?

Rule #4 – When in Doubt, Go Back to the Beginning

- As a leader what movement choices did you make or limit? Why?
- As an individual or a group, did you fall back into old movement biases? Which ones?
- Did you change levels? Why or Why not?
- Did you use only your arms to make shapes, or did you use your whole body?
- Did both feet remain on the floor the whole time? Why or Why not?
- Did you ever invert your verticality?

All of these questions are meant to push our students to think bigger and broader. While safety is always paramount, you will notice that as complexity and new situations are presented, your students will fall back into old movement habits.

Armed with this new information, instruct your students to return to their groups and repeat the exercise. After some time has elapsed, return to the debriefing circle and discuss what new items were discovered.

As your students continue to grow in this exercise, you can complicate it by changing the following items:

- Instead of groups of three, have groups of four dancers. This time, the students will stand in a diamond shape. Person A will be the leader/top point of the diamond (facing away from the group), Persons B and C will be the sides of the diamond (facing the back of Person A), and Person D will be the bottom point of the diamond (facing the back of Person A). The exercise remains the same but with an additional person who can now be the leader.
- The most complicated version of this exercise consists of five dancers per group. In this version, four dancers create a diamond shape, and the fifth person stands in the middle of the diamond. The reason this complicates the exercise is because as the group passes the leadership, Person 5 will always be in a place where he/she/they can take the leadership position. If/when Person 5 takes leadership, this means that at least one person will have their back to Person 5 – making it extremely hard to mirror them. In this instance, the person with their back to Person 5 should use their peripheral vision to follow the person to their right or left, never fully knowing if they are actually mirroring Person 5.

- The final version of this exercise allows members in each group (regardless if they are a leader or a follower) to begin mirroring members from other groups. The first phase of this version requires any member from one group deciding to mirror the movements of another group to remain with their original group. She/he/they can, in turn, continue to mirror a different group, or they can also choose to return to mirroring their own group's leader. Finally, you may allow students to physically leave their original group should they decide to mirror another group. In this case, the student merely walks over to the group she/he/they desire to mirror and takes an open space available. This will, in turn, cause the various groups to morph in shape and size, thus increasing the need for adaptability, compromise, and proprioception.

Exercise #4: Negative Space Exploration

This exercise is meant to build on the skills introduced thus far (decision making, impulse, executing on opportunity, and safety), while also introducing the idea of sharing a communal and equitable working space with another individual. It begins much like the mirror exercise from Chapter 5 but advances beyond the mirror exercise fairly quickly. It may also be helpful at this time to define negative space.

Negative space is quite simply all of the empty space that surrounds/exists between an object or objects. If you geek out on physics like I do, you could make the argument that such space does not exist: understanding that even our air is made up for many imperceptible molecules and atoms. Therefore, for the sake of this exercise, negative space is all of the perceivable empty space that exists around and in between an object and/or objects.

Separate your students into pairs. Instruct them to pick a Person A and a Person B. In order to avoid this taking too much time, simply count down from "5" out loud. This will force your students to make a decision quickly without having time to assign some preconceived, binary notion of what A and B could mean. Once they have picked their letter, instruct them to face one another in their pairs.

Person A will stand in what I call the Vitruvian Man.[1] More simply put, Person A stands in an X shape. Instruct Person B to now begin exploring the negative space around Person A. After some time, have them switch roles so

Rule #4 – When in Doubt, Go Back to the Beginning

that Person B is standing in an X position and Person A is exploring the negative space around Person B.

After switching roles several times, gather the students into the debriefing circle for discussion. Ask your students these following questions:

- What negative space did you explore?
- What negative space did you not explore? Why?
- How did you explore the negative space? Did you use only your arms to explore the space? Why?
- What other parts of our body can we explore the negative space with?
- What parts of our body are we uncomfortable exploring the negative space with? Why?
- While exploring the negative space, did you change levels?

Armed with this new information, have the students repeat the exercise. This time however, allow them to determine when they wish to change between the Vitruvian Man and the Negative Space Explorer.

Instruct Person A to start as the Vitruvian Man. She/he/they can now begin to slowly change the negative space around them by changing the shape of their arms, legs, torso, etc. Person B is to explore the ever-changing negative space until she/he/they desire to be the negative space maker. In much the same way discussed in the original mirror exercise, the dancers portraying the Vitruvian Man should be trying to take care of the Negative Space Explorer by moving slowly enough to remove any worry of physical injury or mental fatigue.

At first, the students in each pair may pause mid exercise to establish role changes. However, when this occurs, encourage them to not start over but simply pause in whatever shape they are in and then continue from there.

The final progression of this exercise leans further into what the students learned in the original mirror exercise: to be able to communicate with one another without having to use words or physical indications. In other words, this final iteration (when done well) should be fluid and without pauses so that an outside observer cannot tell who is the Vitruvian Man and who is the Negative Space Explorer. Put another way, when done to its fullest, both dancers are simultaneously playing the shape maker and the shape explorer.

Rule #4 – When in Doubt, Go Back to the Beginning

Citation

1 Leonardo da Vinci's drawing based on two superimposed images of a man with his arms and legs in two separate positions. The man is centered both within a circle and square.

Notes

Rule #5 – The Moment You Check Out, Someone Gets Hurt

Introduction

Much has been said and written in human history as it relates to caring for others. Many religions and faith practices around the world discuss the idea of neighbor, brother, and friend, and many poets, authors, and artists have created works meant to address the idea of "being my brother's keeper." Similarly, throughout human history, there have been times where cultural revolutions and global conflicts have caused us to pause and investigate our interconnectedness as humans.

It is important to note that only since the last chapter have your students been working in a more communal setting (i.e. working with a partner and/or being able to move mirroring groups) via this book's suggested curriculum. Most of their development has been on self-improvisation and movement generation. While this portion of learning dance improvisation never changes, as we will always be discovering new personal biases and habits, eventually community and larger, group-based dance improvisations must be a part of training. Not only do more bodies in space create more opportunity for inspiration and stimuli (i.e. the cycle of improvisation becomes more complex), but learning how to navigate and adapt one's own personal exploration within the context of a greater community creates a more mature and balanced improviser.

Context

It is important for young dancers to both understand and learn that dance improvisation is not merely doing whatever they want, whenever they want. A lifetime of self-driven movement exploration leaves little room for the joy and inspiration that can come from a communal experience and reduces the potential for multiple points of inspiration and learning. Different dancers and movers move differently, and it is the experience of sharing space with others that further allows us as individuals to break out of our own biases. Additionally, by learning that one's own actions have multiple reactions, a young dancer can learn to both lead and follow in a dance setting.

This understanding is keenly needed as a part of a performer's arsenal. Also, it is simply unsafe to ignore the world around oneself. As more and more bodies are added to a space, the more and more each improviser/dancer must become aware of their surroundings and the affect their actions have on the others sharing the space. More often than not, if someone is injured during an improvisation it is because either she/he/they checked out, or someone in the same space checked out. Dance improvisation requires that participants remain in a constant state of alertness, being always open for new stimuli/impulses, while simultaneously always being aware of all others in the space. Imagine what the world could be like if we learned this as humans.

As a part of understanding how one's actions affect others, it is important to first understand that all persons possess histories that dictate how each of them is affected. One such history (and perhaps one of the largest I would argue) is that of, what I call, **Touch History**. Touch History is a collective dictionary we each have built in our own minds and bodies regarding what being touched (both in general and specific) means to us. Likewise, we have built a second dictionary on how to touch others based on what we are trying to signal when we touch them. This Touch History is something that must be both investigated and relearned before we can begin to truly be our brother's keeper.

Though it is one of the great universals of the human race, the act and sensation of physical touch has been hijacked throughout human history, and more to the point, in current American culture. Touch in the current American commercial culture is mainly used as a means of capital marketing, power dynamic, sexual advertising, and fantasizing. American culture is saturated with messages and suggestions on what physical touch is, means, and how to accomplish it. Many times these suggestions have little, if nothing, to do with actual physical contact, but rather some hidden message behind that touch. This ultimately leaves individuals in a space where touch can, and does, mean multiple things. Throw onto this any historic experiences we each individually may have with touch (good or bad), and it isn't hard to see why physical contact is such a heightened experience for many of our students.

This historic weight inevitably creeps its way into our dance studios and classes, and therefore must be addressed if we are to open additional forms of

Non-Biological External Impulses for our students. While it would be ideal for us to be able to wave a magic wand and simply make all of the challenges surround physical touch go away, the truth is that we cannot. Likewise, neither can we be our students' therapists. However, what we can do is begin to guide them in a safe and healthy manner toward the idea of how physical touch can be used in dance in a manner that is both nontoxic and, simultaneously, inspiring. Before I present some exercises, let me first break down some of the ways in which we as humans explore the physical world through touch, and how these somatic biases inherently affect both our communication skills and our relationship to touch.

Considerations

The first item to recognize is that a majority of our adult lives have been spent exploring the physical world with our hands. There are both evolutionary and safety reasons for this, but, above all, exploring the physical world through our hands is the most efficient manner of interaction. Not only do our hands reach further from our bodies than other appendages (making it easier to keep unknown objects at a distance), but our hands also have more dexterity (generally speaking) than most other parts of our bodies. We are able to grab, pull, push, entangle, and handle objects with our hands much easier than other body parts; and since much of evolution is about finding the path of least resistance, we have developed an intrinsic bias toward physical exploration with our hands.

Because of these biases, many individuals have developed emotions, sensations, and assumptions around being touch by someone else's' hand/s. Similarly, because hands are the common physical source for exploration, many people tend to shy away from accepting touch from other body parts, ultimately reducing the possibility for alternative physical stimuli.

While our inclination to explore the world with our hands makes sense from a biological viewpoint, little, if anything, in biology is concerned with advancement of the imagination. Therefore, if we are to expand our imaginations and creativity, we must push against our biology and seek alternative ways of interacting with the physical world. This means we must first understand that there are many more physical ways to experience the world than simply with our hands.

A simple online search reveals that the human skin is the largest organ the body possesses and replenishes itself (depending on one's age) approximately every 27–48 days. Imagine how much potential this statement possesses! If our entire body's outer layer replenishes every month or so, how much of the world are we missing by experiencing it only through our hands? Better yet, what new ideas and ways of creating could we come up with if we were to explore and experience life with parts of our bodies that are much more sensitive? The possibilities could be limitless if we are only willing to take the path less traveled and begin first by allowing ourselves the joy (and dare I say freedom) of experiencing this physical world with all of our body, rather than a finite portion of it.

A second item worth discussing is clothing. While I certainly am not about to suggest nudity as a cure for a culture's bias toward physical touch, I do wish to point out that clothing has developed (particularly in the United States) as a means of giving signals and messages surrounding skin, touch, personality, identity, and the supposed desired outcomes of our clothing choices. Isn't it interesting that certain locations/environments are considered acceptable for less clothing, and other locations/environments are not? While some of this does have to do with items such as weather, climate, etc., some of it also deals with cultural norms surrounding what access to skin means and doesn't mean. Likewise, it seems fascinating that showing more skin is reserved for locations where we are encouraged to be more care-free, relaxed, and innocent, whereas locations with less skin are deemed serious, corporate, and mature.

What signals are we sending to ourselves and those around us based on these ideas? More importantly, when do we feel most creative, inspired, and aware of fully being alive? Perhaps one could argue that we feel better in places with more skin showing because they are inherently warmer (the beach), we are on vacation (a cruise), and/or we are in a communal setting (a friend's house). Perhaps that is only part of the equation. Couldn't it also be that because we have less clothing on at these times we are also experiencing more of the world via multiple points of physical contact, and therefore we are inherently more inspired due to our heighted sense of self and our physical environment? All this being said, clothing (be it through marketing or the wearing of) has contributed to our understanding and innate reaction to physical touch, and therefore it is important to understand that much of our skin is not used for experiencing the physical world – let along another human being.

A final point of discussion is the actual act of touching. While we would all like to think that we are capable of interacting physically with our world in a manner that is benign, the reality is that every time we touch something or someone we do so with an intention and desired outcome. When we sit in a chair there is an inherent expectation that that chair will support our weight; and

Rule #5 – The Moment You Check Out, Someone Gets Hurt

we are surprised when the chair doesn't hold up to its end of the bargain. When we extend our hand to say hello, we assume that the other person will extend their hand. When we extend our arms for a hug, we do so with the full intention of hugging someone else. When we place our hand on a student to give a correction, we do so with the intention to give them guidance. When we reach for a glass of water, we intend to pick it up, consuming its contents, and then placing it back down. There are millions of these interactions in our daily routines, and therefore we have built a lifetime of touching with intention.

The problem this causes is that it is extremely difficult to physically interact with our world in a manner that states, "I am touching you with no purpose other than to experience this moment." Stated differently, when was the last time you touched something for the sole purpose of simply experiencing it? Furthermore, if you were to do this with another human being, what do you think would be the reaction of the person you are now touching? The fact of the matter is that touch has become something more than what it is: simply a touch. Therefore, as a part of this training we must slowly (and again I stress slowly) introduce our students to the idea of both touching and being touched without intention. Only then can physical contact, like many other external stimuli, serve as a source of inspiration and impulse for movement generation, rather than a hindrance that stifles both our imaginations.

Try

Exercise #1: Guiding Your Fellow Dancer

This exercise is fairly straight forward. Have the students pair up.

- Now is the time to start watching if certain dancers keep pairing up with the same individuals (i.e. their friends).
- If you see this happening, adjust how you have your students pair up. You could of course simply assign them their pairs, but eventually we want our students choosing their partner in a manner that they actually (given the choice) choose someone who isn't their best friend.
- Another option is to repeat the machine game from Chapter 4. However, once the machine is built assign them to a partner based on the order they added to the machine.

- You may also choose any other manner in which you feel will diversify each student's partner selection.

Once the students have been paired up, again ask them to pick a Person A and a Person B.

- Once chosen, tell all of the students who are identifying as Person A to close their eyes.
- Now instruct all of the students identifying as Person B to take the partner (Person A) by the hand.
- Person B will now lead their partner throughout the room while Person A's eyes remain closed. Once they have accomplished this task for a while, have them switch.
- Person A will now lead Person B by the hand throughout the room while Person B keeps their eyes closed.

A few items to consider:

- Remind the students that this is yet another time to earn the trust of their fellow dancers, and that **trust is very hard to earn back once it is lost**.
- Now is not the time for the person who is leading to laugh. The student who is being lead with their eyes closed may laugh out of fear and/or nervousness, and this is acceptable. However, the person leading must show the person following that he/she/they take the leadership role seriously, and therefore will focus all of their efforts on being a safe leader.
- Remind the person who is being led to relax and soften their muscles. Remind them that tight muscles expose joints and bones, and joints hurt more to bump into than soft muscle.

Once all students have been both the leader and the follower, circle them all up for discussion. Ask them the following questions:

- How did it feel to be lead with your eyes closed? Why do you think you felt that way?
- What were you thinking about as the leader? Where you only focusing on what was in front of you, or were you considering that the person you were

Rule #5 – The Moment You Check Out, Someone Gets Hurt

leading had additional obstacles (i.e. all the other people in the room who may be coming in from the sides or back)?

- As a leader, did you walk forward with your hand behind you, or did you walk backward so you were facing your partner the whole time? Why? What are the pros and cons to each approach?
- What cues could you identify from the person leading in order to help guide you as the follower?
- What other senses kicked in that either aided you in walking with your eyes closed, or made you nervous?
- What did you learn about yourself during this exercise? What will you focus on next time in order to make the task easier?

With the debriefing completed, have the students pair up with their same partner and complete the task again.

Once all students have been both the leader and the follower, have them change partners. You may repeat the machine game again as a means of ensure a diversified pairing, or you can choose any other method you prefer. Again, ultimately you want them to start choosing their partners, and doing so in a manner that reflects their understanding of the need to experience working with as many people as possible.

Once all students have been both the leader and the follower in their new pair, circle them all up for discussion. Ask them the following questions:

- What was different about working with someone new? What was similar?
- Did the person leading you this time have different cues to follow than your previous partner?
- As the leader, how did you act differently working with a new partner? What knowledge did you gain working with this new person?

You can repeat this exercise as many times as necessary in order to see growth in the students as it relates to (a) the leaders taking great care with their responsibility of leading, and (b) the person following giving all control to the person leading.

Once your students have successfully completed this exercise multiple times, you can now begin to add complexity by doing the following:

- Consider having the person who is leading increase the tempo at which they are walking. If you choose to do this, you will want to reduce the number

of people actually executing the exercise: more bodies equal more opportunity for collision.
- Consider asking the leader to start leading the follower by holding onto a different part of the body than the hand. Consider holding the follower's shoulder, elbow, or waist. This may mean some adaptation on behalf of the leader.
- Consider asking the leader to "lead from behind," rather than from the front. She/he/they can (for example) put their hands on the follower's hips, and guide them through space by pushing them, rather than pulling.
- Consider adding vertical dynamics. You will notice that the leaders will tend to remain standing the whole time while guiding. Ask the leaders to change their vertical levels as they maneuver through space with their partner. You may ask the same of the followers.
- Consider asking the leaders to make contact with the followers through a different part of their bodies other than their hands. For example, the leader could have her/his/their elbow touching the follower's forearm. In order for the task to be accomplished, both the leader and the follower will have to focus on maintaining physical contact at the point of touch. This aids in the process of teaching the students that other parts of the body can lead and be led other than just the hands.

Exercise #2: Across the Floor No Two Ways the Same in a Partner's Negative Space

This exercise is a continuation of Exercise #4 from Chapter 6, and it is a continuation of proprioceptive awareness.

- Return to the Across the Floor Exercise No Two Ways the Same exercise from Chapter 3.
- It may be worth simply performing this exercise several times with various constraints as a refresher for your students.
- After having done this refresher, you will ask your students to pair up.
- As a reminder, try to avoid having your students pair up with their closest friends.

Once your students have paired up and have relocated to one side of the room/studio, have three or four pairs step forward.

Rule #5 – The Moment You Check Out, Someone Gets Hurt

- Similar to the original exercise, Person A in the exercise will begin to move from one side of the studio to the other in a manner that does not repeat movements or shapes. However, unlike the original version of this exercise, Person A will specifically make and hold a shape.
- While Person A holds the shape, Person B will move toward Person A and, once reaching them, improvise through/around Person A's negative space – thus putting Person B ahead of Person A.
- Once past Person A, Person B will hold a shape, and Person A will travel toward Person B – repeating the negative space improvisation and pausing to hold a shape once past Person B.
- This process continues in a leap frog manner until the pair has successfully made it across the room.
- The next pair waiting to perform the exercise will act as the referees, ensuring that the first pair does not repeat a shape or movement. As with the original exercise, if a pair does repeat, then they must start over from the beginning.

Once all pairs have successfully made it across the floor, have each pair repeat the exercise going back in the other direction.

A few items to consider:

- When first having the students attempt this new adaptation of the exercise, remind them to move slowly. The lesson for this chapter is being aware of others and the need for intentional mindfulness. Moving slowly keeps this exercise safe. This is an awareness I find they are in constant need of reminding.
- After the students begin to get comfortable with their partners, you may now begin to add constraints to the exercise. As a reminder, these confinements can be based on shape (hop and make a new shape each time), vertical levels (high, medium, low), texture (sharp, round, soft, angular, etc.), time (fast, slow, 20 seconds to get across the floor, etc.), and/or points of contact with the floor (e.g. only three points of contact at any point in time).
- The most advanced version of this exercise eliminates the leap frog sensation by asking the students to simply improvise within each other's negative space while ensuring that all movement is continuous as they move forward in space.

Exercise #3: Reintroducing Touch

This exercise is perhaps one of the most important of this curriculum, and therefore it is an exercise that should be done multiple times over the course of many classes and weeks. Additionally, if ever there was a time to "take it slow," now is that time.

This exercise is designed to reintroduce your students to the idea of touch, and what touch does, or doesn't, mean. You may discover that your very young dancers (11 years and younger) have little to no hesitancy with this exercise, while your older dancers struggle with it. My theory behind this is that our young dancers haven't been introduced yet to societies messages surrounding touch, and therefore they are closer to understanding a world where physical touch does not possess the cultural baggage that older dancers may possess. Because of this, I recommend reserving this exercise for your oldest and most mature dancers.

Take great care in making sure you move slowly with each step of this exercise, and that you remain in active conversation with your students through the entire exercise. You may want to establish some form of consent and/or safe words that students may choose to use during the duration of this exercise. Additionally, you know your dancers best. If there is a student or students who has experiences some sort of physical trauma, then this may not be the time or place to introduce this exercise. Simply put, you should be intentionally engaged and verbally guiding your students during this exercise should you feel comfortable introducing it. Your continual vocal guidance and mental engagement not only reassures them of the safety of the space, but also gives them the permission to begin to release any walls they may have built up regarding physical touch.

If done well, this exercise has the potential to rewrite how your dancers view and interaction with physical touch. This exercise can set them up for greater partnering skills in the future, and can begin to unravel some of the fears they may have regarding touch in dance. Therefore, I encourage you to not spring this exercise onto your students in class. Give your dancers plenty of warning several classes before so that any student who may be struggling with touch can speak with you well in advance and in a private/safe space.

I will state it once more: you know your students best and therefore you may need to adapt this exercise to fit the unique needs of each dancer/group of dancers.

Begin by having the students pair up.

- Again, if you feel it necessary you can choose their partners for them, or use any number of pairing exercises you desire in order to achieve a diversified partnering situation.
- As always, have each pair pick a Person A and Person B.
- Once the labels have been assigned, Person B will sit in what I refer to as the Safe Position. This position is accomplished by having a person sit on the floor, their knees are slightly bent so they can rest their arms on their knees, legs slightly open so as to supply support, the back is slightly hunched over, and the head is relaxed and placed in the space between arms and knees. This position allows Person B to remain seated in a relaxed and supported position that can be maintained for several minutes while their eyes remain closed. This position also maintains a certain amount of protection of the front of the body, as well as any areas of the body that a student may feel is vulnerable or intimate.

With Person B now seated in the safe position with their eyes closed, instruct Person A to kneel beside Person B. Person A may now begin to touch Person B on various parts of their body. Before you begin this exercise, consider the following:

- Instruct the person who is doing the touching to start with their hand. As discussed, the hand is a familiar object for contact.
- Instruct the person doing the touching to keep their hand as soft and neutral as possible.
  - Remind the person doing the touching to refrain from placing too much or too little weight on the person being touched.
  - Leave the hand in contact with a specific body part for some time, allowing the person who is being touched to accept the touch.
  - This longer period of physical contact allows the person doing the touching time needed in order to experience this acceptance. Part of this exercise is re-teaching our students/dancers how to touch without any intention.
- Instruct the person who is being touched to focus on the touch itself. Do not focus on where they are being touched, but rather what physical senses are experienced in the touch (i.e. heat, weight, texture, electricity, etc.). Part of this exercise is also teaching our dancers/students how to accept touch as nothing more than an opportunity for creativity and inspiration.

Rule #5 – The Moment You Check Out, Someone Gets Hurt

- Instruct the person doing the touching to start with areas that are familiar and exposed:
  - The shoulders, the upper back, the middle back, the lower back, the shins and ankles of the legs, the forearms, wrists and hands, and the top and back of the head.
  - All of these areas are already exposed in the safe position, and therefore prevent any undesired bumps or shoves that may occur trying to make contact with a part of the body that isn't exposed.
  - These are also parts of the body that are generally used to being in contact with items in our daily lives, and therefore do not prevent as much of a shock when being touched by the person initiating contact.
- Continually coach 3your students throughout this process. I refer to this process as "building the **Tactile Encyclopedia**." The ability to know where to touch a fellow dancer without having to always see that body part, or the ability to know what body part is being touched without having to see it, is a skill fundamental to successful partnering. Thus, not only does this exercise reintroduce dancers to physical touch, but it also begins to build an actual tactile map of the human body.
- Try to remember what you say during your coaching so you can repeat it when the students switch positions with their partners.
- Encourage the person doing the touching to close their eyes once they have made contact. This too is a way to begin building their tactile encyclopedia.
- Remind all participants that this is yet again another time to build trust. While some laughing may be permitted, I generally discourage it.

  After some time has lapsed (generally 7–10 minutes), instruct the person who is doing the touching to initiate contact one last time. This will be the last time they touch Person B, after which they are to sit beside their partner as a sign of completing the exercise. Once all individuals who are initiating contact are completed, instruct the students to debrief/converse with their partner.
- I generally do not bring the whole class together for debriefing at this moment, as I feel it is important that each partner group have a chance to bond over the experience.
- After some time has passed, instruct the students in their pairs to switch. Person A will now be the person in the safe position, and Person B will now be the person touching.

Rule #5 – The Moment You Check Out, Someone Gets Hurt

- Coach this section of the exercise exactly as you did the first section, ensuring your inflection, comments, and guidance remains as similar as possible.

    Once the exercise has been completed, ask the students in the pairs to discuss again. Once you sense these conversations winding down, you may now gather the class as a whole to discuss and debrief.

    Consider asking the following questions:

- As the person being touched, what did you notice as time went on? Even though your eyes were closed, what other senses could you use to experience the touch?
- As the person doing the touching, what did you find easy about this exercise, and what did you find difficult? Why?
- As the person being touched, were there some parts of your body that were more sensitive to touch than others? Why do you think this is?
- As the person doing the touching, did you feel more comfortable touching some parts of the body, and less comfortable with other parts? Why do you think that is?
- As the person being touched, could you start to guess where the person who was touching you was going to make contact? Were you right in your guess? What could lead to this?
- As the person doing the touching, what different sensations (i.e. textures, heat, energy) did you experience based on the various body parts you touched? How can these indicators aid you in building your tactile encyclopedia?

After debriefing with the entire class have the students return to their original pairs and complete the entire exercise again. Once completed, bring the class together again to discuss how the second time performing this exercise was different than the first. Feel free to add additional questions to this debriefing section based on what you observed.

Following debriefing, have the students change their partners and repeat the exercise. You will want to have your students complete the entire exercise with at least three to four different partners before moving on to the next progression of this exercise.

The following is a list of the progressive levels for this exercise:

I. **Progression I:** Touching body placements that are not as easily exposed in the safe position, as well as adding multiple points of contact. One example might be using two hands at the same time: placing one hand on a shoulder and the other hand on the thigh.

II. **Progression II:** Return to touching only the exposed body parts in the safe position, but this time with a different body part than the hand (e.g. the person doing the touching initiates contact with their elbow instead of their hand)

III. **Progression III:** Touching body placements that are not as easily exposed in the safe position with a different body part than the hand.

IV. **Progression IV:** Touching only the exposed body parts in the safe position, but this time with multiple different body parts other than the hands.

V. **Progression V:** Touching body parts that are not as easily exposed in the safe position with different body parts other than the hand/hands.

For each of the progressions, be sure to follow the same format as the original exercise:

- Multiple chances to work with the same partner.
- Multiple chances to work with a different partner.
- Debriefing in pairs as well as the entire class.
- Continued verbal coaching are all essential aspects to maintain with each progression.

Following the completion of all progressions, you may now begin to change the resting position of the person being touched. The following is the progressive resting positions the person being touched will take:

I. The safe position but with the head up, which exposes the neck and throat.
II. Lying face down on the floor in an open "X" position.
   a. An added progression for this position is allowing the person doing the touching to lay their entire body on top of the person lying on the floor.
      i. First have the person doing the touching lay the backside of their body across/on top of the backside of the person being touched.
      ii. Second, have the person doing the touching lay the front half of their body across/on top of the backside of the person being touched.
III. Lying on the right side of the body with their arms at their sides.
IV. Lying on the left side of the body with their arms at their sides.

V. Lying face up on the floor with their knees bent and feet flat on the floor.

VI. Lying face up on the floor in an open "X" position.
   a. An added progression for this position is allowing the person doing the touching to lay their entire body on top of the person lying on the floor.
      i. First have the person doing the touching lay the backside of their body across/on top of the front half of the person being touched.
      ii. Second, have the person doing the touching lay the front half of their body across/on top of the front half of the person being touched

For each of the resting positions, be sure to <u>always</u> start from the beginning of the exercise (i.e. one hand on one body part). Depending how often you instruct this class, this exercise could take weeks or even months to complete. Take as much time as needed, returning to the beginning as often as you need. Continually remind the students that the goal of this exercise is to

- Learn how to touch without intention.
- Learn how to receive touch without intention.
- Build a tactile vocabulary both as the person being touched and the person doing the touching.

By continually focusing on the actual goals of the exercise, we assist our students in overcoming any nervousness they may feel.

Notes

Rule #6 – It Takes a Village to Raise an Improvisation

Introduction

With Chapter 7, we began to introduce our students to the idea of caring for one another, as well as diving deeper into practices and exercises that involve multiple participants. However, we have not yet actually begun to incorporate full communal/large group dance improvisations as a part of the course work. While improvising individually can be both cathartic and energizing, eventually it can run the risk of becoming self-indulgent and limiting. Yes, improvisation is a personal journey (of sorts), but it is also made fullest when experienced in a community. Like rich conversation with friends over a glass (or two) of wine, communal improvisation opens practitioners to new ways of thinking, reacting, and moving. Simultaneously, communal improvisation prevents the risk of assuming dance improvisation is only about "what I want" and forces practitioners to see a greater world beyond that which they have created for themselves.

Context

It is worth taking a moment to pause and recognize that the idea of community may be something different for you the teacher than for your students. For those like me who grew up having actual playground time during the school day, hanging at friends' houses during summer, and generally being around people when I was bored, the idea of community is attached to physical proximity to others. However, today's young dancers understand community vastly different.

In a world of social media, text messaging, and a host of applications that "connect us," our students see community not as those with whom they are physically present, but rather a self-selected and highly filtered cohort of people

DOI: 10.4324/9781003387084-9

with whom they commune via technology. Isn't it fascinating that in today's context the understanding of community and communication is akin, if not relegated to, character limits, emojis, and GIFs? Perhaps more to the point, what is lost when our students understanding of conversation, community, and engagement is tied to a lack of physical contact with others? I would argue that physical community and its understanding is, perhaps, needed even more today.

Fear not, this chapter will not turn into a long diatribe concerning the woes of technology and "kids these days," rather it merely addresses the fact that a teacher's understanding and experience of community/village is vastly different than that of her/his/their students. There is a very real and present need for our students to fully understand the meaning and experience of immediately present community, and the joys and complexities that come with physical presence. In this setting, one must learn how to look, listen, adapt, compromise, lead, follow, and discover how he/she/they fit within the community as well as how they may contribute to its continuation, or, perhaps, change its trajectory if needed. Therefore, the practice, training, and skill building of dance improvisation within a community have far reaching results that extend well beyond the classroom.

It is also worth taking a few moments to refer back to the Cycle of Improvisation discussed in Chapter 1. An important part of this cycle is both the change made to the environment in reaction to a physical decision, and the adaptation needed in order to accommodate this new change. Nothing creates the urgency for adaptation like additional bodies in space. These bodies are independent entities that cannot be controlled by any singular individual, and therefore act and react in ways that are unpredictable and instantaneous. What a wonderful skillset for our students to learn: the ability to physically and directly interact with others whom they have not had the privilege of self-selecting.

While we may argue that dancers in general already have this skill due to dancing in a work created by a choreographer, I would suggest that this is a very different experience. A piece of choreography generally has a singular person at the helm (i.e. the choreographer). In other words, items such as choice-making, chance, unpredictability, and agency are rarely used as a part of the final product in a dance performance. On the contrary, these items are very much avoided out of fear that their unpredictability will hinder the consistency needed for performances. However, in an improvisational setting these items are not only inherent, they are, in a sense, the very nature of the thing. Therefore, students who learn to master the ability to physically commune within a given village are that much more attuned to nuance, adaptability, and empathetic reaction. I would argue that these are all items we as teachers and choreographers desire of our dancers.

Considerations

One final thought before we dive into exercises:

Adding community builds and increases creativity.

In a later chapter we will discuss the idea of external stimuli and its place in dance improvisation. However, right now I would simply like to focus on the idea of walking a mile in someone else's shoes. As the saying suggests, an individual must experience the life and circumstances of another human being in order to fully grasp the reasons a particular person sees, understands, and experiences life in a particular manner. In other words, in order to build empathy, we must live as another has lived. Ironically, this idea also has its application in dance improvisation.

As we have discussed, each of us has our own physical biases based on our culture, sex, sexual identity, gender identity, race, ethnicity, religious beliefs, and a host of other forces pressing upon us. While we have spent the first half of this book working to undo these biases, nothing can free us faster, and with more ease, than living in someone else's skin. Physically-proximal improvisational communities do this for us. They force us to physically take on the somatic mannerisms and executions of those who surround us. This physical empathy (as it were) allows us to experience the world in a manner that is completely foreign to our way of moving. It gives us a launching pad from which to catapult new ways of shape making, locomotion, and dance making.

In short, our improvisational village grants us the opportunity to not only expand our own movement vocabulary, but readily supplies us with a real-time Human Movement Buffet from which to partake.

Try

Exercise #1: Across the Floor No Two Ways the Same, but Mirroring/Shadowing a Partner

This first exercise addresses the idea of living in someone else's skin.
Return to the Across the Floor Exercise No Two Ways the Same exercise.

Once your students have paired up and relocated to one side of the room/studio, have three or four pairs step forward.

- Similar to the original exercise, Person A in the exercise will begin to move from one side of the studio to the other in a manner that does not repeat movements or shapes. However, unlike the original version of this exercise, Person A will only move a few feet in space before stopping.
- Once Person A has stopped, Person B will now move toward Person A executing, to the best of their ability, the exact same steps/movement that Person A produced in order to travel.
- Once Person B has arrived to Person A, Person A will once again travel a few more feet (no two ways the same) while Person B observes.
- After a few feet of traveling, Person A will stop and Person B must once again reproduce the steps of Person A.

This exercise continues until both Person A and Person B are on the other side of the room. Once the first line has made it across the room, it is time for the second line (i.e. second set of paired students) to accomplish the same task.

Once all students have made it across the floor, repeat the exercise going back the other way, but have Person B be the leader and Person A be the follower/mimic.

A few items to consider:

- When first having the students attempt this new adaptation of the exercise, remind them to move slowly.
  - Similar to other exercises in this book, it is hard to retain and execute someone else's movement if the movement tempo is too quick.
  - Also, allow all levels and no constraints at first. This allows the students the freedom to move as they see fit without the added pressure of meeting expectations defined by level, texture, or time.
- After several passes across the floor, ask the leader to increase the distance they travel before stopping. This will challenge the follower/mimicker to retain more and "live in the skin" of the leader for longer periods of time.
  - Eventually the leader should cross the entire floor before the follower/mimic executes the leader's movements.
  - You can increase the difficulty of the leader by asking them to remember their sequence of movements. This allows the leader to then observe

Rule #6 – It Takes a Village to Raise an Improvisation

the follower and tell him/her/they (i.e. the follower) to go back to the beginning if he/she/they miss a step the leader performed.

- You can actually introduce this early in the exercise as a means of challenging the leader and follower/mimic. This requirement that the leader build a physical memory of their improvised actions is a skill we will discuss later in this book, but for now, this is a great introduction to this skill.

- After the students begin to get comfortable with their partners, you may now begin to add constraints to the person leading.
  - As a reminder, these constraints can be based on shape (hop and make a new shape each time), vertical levels (high, medium, low), texture (sharp, round, soft, angular, etc.), time (fast, slow, 20 seconds to get across the floor, etc.), and/or points of contact with the floor (e.g. only three points of contact at any point in time).

- Each time you perform this task in a new class session, be sure to have your students change partners. This forces them to learn and adapt to movement styles of all their peers, not just a selected handful.

After a full pass (i.e. both Person A and Person B have been the leader), collect the class for discussion/debriefing. Here are a few suggested questions to spur conversation:

- What did you first notice about yourself when you tried to mimic your partner's movement?
- What made it difficult to mimic your partner?
- What made it easier to mimic your partner?
- What was different about the way your partner moved from the way you normally move?
- What was challenging about memorizing your movement as a leader?
- What could make it easier to remember your movement? How might this impact your ability to improvise versus creating planned movement?
- How might we improvise and still remember our movement?
- How can we begin to incorporate others' movement preferences into our own movement practice?

Rule #6 – It Takes a Village to Raise an Improvisation

Between each new progression of this exercise, be sure to gather the class for discussion and debriefing. You may develop additional questions as you observe the class, but feel free to use the above questions as a starting point.

Exercise #2: Moving Toward and Away from Touch

Before you begin this exercise be sure that your students have accomplished ALL six progressions of Exercise #3 from Chapter 7. Not until all of your students execute these progressions with confidence, respect, and comfort should you move onto this exercise. If you move to this exercise too early you run the risk of reinforcing old biases regarding touch, and therefore render the work done in Chapter 7 meaningless. It is for this reason I stressed that the touch exercise may take months before completed, especially if you have dance improvisation classes only once or twice a week as a part of your curriculum.

This exercise continues the idea of reintroducing touch, and the personal agency that can come with it. Once again have your students pair up, picking a Person A and a Person B. As a side note, by this time in the curriculum your students should be used to the idea of pairing up, how to accomplish it in an efficient manner, and that they are to pick a partner with whom they may not normally spend time.

Once paired up, have the various pairs find space in the classroom/studio.

- Make sure there is plenty of space between the pairs. Approximately a 6-foot diameter around each pair. This may mean some pairs may have to observe at first. If this is the case, this gives a great opportunity for you as an instructor to work with the students who are observing.
- Also, remind the students of the rules regarding touch from Chapter 7. It never hurts to return to previous rules of engagement, as each day is a different day and each student comes to class with a new day's worth of information and context.

Of the pairs still standing, have Person A take the standing Vitruvian Man position (discussed in Chapter 7).

- Person B is now instructed to begin to touch Person A with the palm of their hand.

Rule #6 – It Takes a Village to Raise an Improvisation

- Once touched in/on a location, Person A should move that specific body part toward the touch. I specifically begin with moving toward the touch since this is not always the human inclination.
- As with the touch exercise in Chapter 7, Person B should only touch with the palm of one hand at first, as well as only make contact with one body part of their partner.
- Allow this exercise to continue for some time (10–15 minutes) before switching to Person B taking the Vitruvian Man, and Person A doing the touching.

After each person has been both the Vitruvian Man and the person touching, either switch who is sitting in class and who is participating, or gather the whole class (if everyone has participated) for discussion and debriefing.

A few items to consider:

- While the exercise is going on, speak with the observers (if you have students seated) about what you see, what they see, and what new ideas/lessons they may take from watching. This is great preparation for Chapter 11 where group improvisations will be split into smaller groups with some students improvising and some students observing.
- While observing the students executing this exercise you may notice that some students move toward the touch with more of their body than the part being touched. Remind students that they are, in fact, being asked to move only the body part being touched. This accomplished two items:
    I. It forces the person being touched to learn how to move their body in isolation – sometimes requiring critical and lateral thinking. This is intentional as not all body parts move as easily in space as others. This again is a way in which we are training them to expand their movement vocabulary, while training enhanced control of their physical being.
    II. It protects the person doing the touching. If the person doing the touching cannot trust that their partner will move in a manner that is safe for them, he/she/they will inherently refrain from touching certain locations on the body. We want to reduce this from happening since part of these touch exercises is meant to prepare students for partnering and contact improvisation, which require all body locations accessible for proper and safe interaction.
- As with the original touch exercise, there are various levels of this exercise meant to increase both contact and adaptability. Before moving onto each

Rule #6 – It Takes a Village to Raise an Improvisation

level (36 levels in total) ensure that all students can execute each progression with confidence, respect, and comfort. Until this occurs, progressing to the next level should not take place.

- The following are the progressive levels for this exercise. Each level should take approximately 5–10 minutes per person: for a total of 10–20 minutes per pair. This may seem exhaustive, but in truth it is no different than any number of other skills we ask our students to execute and repeat during the course of their training.

  I. One hand at a time moving toward the touch
  II. One hand at a time moving away from the touch
  III. One hand at a time moving toward or away from the touch (Vitruvian Man's choice)
  IV. One hand at a time moving toward the touch based on the weight/pressure of the touch
  V. One hand at a time moving away from the touched based on the weight/pressure of the touch
  VI. One hand at a time moving toward or away from the touch (Vitruvian Man's choice) based on the weight/pressure of the touch
      A. Repeat levels I–VI, but adding two hands/points of contact to the Vitruvian Man
      B. Repeat levels I–VI, but returning to a single point of contact (<u>other than the hands</u>) on the Vitruvian Man
      C. Repeat levels I–VI with two points of contact (other than the hands) on the Vitruvian Man
      D. Repeat levels I–VI with multiple points of contact (more than two) on the Vitruvian Man.

Once the initial level (i.e. one hand at a time moving toward the touch) has been completed by both students in each pair, gather the class as a whole to discuss and debrief. This process should occur after each level progression. Consider asking the following questions for various levels of this exercise:

- Was it hard to move toward the touch? Why or why not? Why do you think this is?
- Was it hard to move away from the touch? Why or why not? Why do you think this is?

Rule #6 – It Takes a Village to Raise an Improvisation

- Was it difficult to isolate some body parts being touched? Which ones? What are some creative solutions to moving these specific body parts?
- As the person doing the touching, did you find yourself shying away from some part of the body? Why or why not? Why do you think this is?
- Was it difficult when two points of contact were added? Why or why not?
- Was it difficult when given the choice to move toward or away from the touch? Why or why not?
- As the person doing the touching, how did you have to adapt when the Vitruvian Man could choose to move either toward or away from the touch? How did this affect your role in the exercise?
- What difference did either of you (Vitruvian Man or person doing the touching) experience once touching with other body parts began? Was it harder or easier to touch and/or react to touch? Why or why not?
- What did you experience when (as a pair) you were able to choose who was leading and who was following? Were you able to find a moment when each of you were doing both simultaneously?

Similar to the mirror exercise, once the students have reached the final level, you as the instructor will cease instructing them to switch between Person A and Person B, and they as a pair will begin to explore who is the Vitruvian Man and who is the person touching seamlessly and without stopping. Eventually they will reach a place where they are both acting as the Vitruvian Man and the person touching.

As a final note for this exercise, remember that the various levels will cross over multiple class periods, weeks, and perhaps even months. Do not rush this process, and remind your students that they are in the beginning stages of this journey, and therefore will repeat many exercises multiple times over the course of their training. At the risk of sounding heavy handed, you can remind your students once again that *dance improvisation is a technique, and therefore requires the same amount of time, energy and repetition as all other forms of dance they are studying.*

Exercise #3: Across the Floor No Two Ways the Same, but Making Points of Contact with a Partner

This exercise is yet another adaptation of the Across the Floor No Two Ways the Same exercise. This time, however, the students are now asked to negotiate

Rule #6 – It Takes a Village to Raise an Improvisation

space while remaining in constant physical contact with their partner. By this point there may be no need to return to the original Across the Floor No Two Ways the Same exercise, but, as always, if you feel your students could benefit from revisiting any of the previous version of this exercise, it never hurts to go back to the beginning (Rule #4).

Once your students have paired up, and have relocated to one side of the room/studio, have three or four pairs step forward to begin the exercise.

- Prior to beginning the exercise, have the students in their pairs pick a singular point of contact.
- Per the rules in this book, I always recommend that students start with what they know (Rule #3), and start from the beginning (Rule #4) Therefore, I recommend that each pair simply hold hands as their singular point of contact.
- From this point on, the exercise is fairly straight forward. Each pair must cross the studio from one side to the other, no two ways the same, while maintaining their point of contact.
- The next pair waiting to go acts as the referee, ensuring that the point of contact remains, and there is no repeated movement.
- As always, if one of these rules is broken, the pair executing the exercise must start over from the beginning.

As with most exercises in this book, there are several progressions to this exercise:

I. Across the Floor No Two Ways the Same with one point of contact (holding hands first)
II. Across the Floor No Two Ways the Same with one point of contact (one person uses their hand to make contact with a different body part of their partner)
III. Across the Floor No Two Ways the Same with one point of contact (neither partner can use their hands to make contact)
IV. Across the Floor No Two Ways the Same one point that can change (contact must always be occurring, however the point of contact can change)
    A. Repeat levels I–IV, but with two points of contact
    B. Repeat levels I–IV but with three points of contact.

A few items to consider:

- After the students begin to get comfortable with their partners, you may now begin to add constraints. As a reminder, these constraints can be based on shape (hop and make a new shape each time), vertical levels (high, medium, low), texture (sharp, round, soft, angular, etc.), time (fast, slow, 20 seconds to get across the floor, etc.).
- Each time you perform this task in a new class session, be sure to have your students change partners.

It may be unnecessary to have a class discussion/debriefing session between each level progression, but I do recommend having discussion (at the very least) every time the class moves from a level IV progression to a new level I (adding more points of contact).

Consider the following questions as possible discussion prompts:

- What challenges did you face as you changed points of contact? How did you overcome them?
- How did each progression add both new challenges and new opportunities?
- What new ways of moving did you discover with each progression?
- What limitations do you feel you currently possess that affected your ability to accomplish the exercise?

Notes

Rule #7 – The Hardest Part Isn't Knowing When to Start: It's Knowing How to Start

Introduction

By this time in the curriculum, your students will be well versed in the various exercises, methodologies, and techniques of improvising in their own personal space, within close proximity to other individuals, as well as using and accepting touch merely as a source of inspiration. However, larger group dance improvisations have yet to be explored, as well as the basic conversation regarding how and when to begin a dance improvisation.

This chapter will address this from both a practical and pedagogical viewpoint. However, before we begin to discuss exercises and approaches to guiding your students into the process of beginning a group dance improvisation, it is worth taking some time to explain the reasons for dance improvisation and the tools that allow for dance improvisations to be more cohesive and focused experiences.

Context

Let's discuss what, for me, are the three main purposes of dance improvisation. While there are many reasons for, and expectations of, dance improvisation, I have found the following three categories as helpful identifiers by which to discuss dance improvisation and guide students on beginning an improvisation. These three purposes are

(1) Dance Improvisation for Movement Generation.
(2) Dance Improvisation in a Performance.
(3) Dance Improvisation as a Performance.

DOI: 10.4324/9781003387084-10

These three categories (though broad) assist us as instructors, as well as our students, to find entry points into the conversations surrounding dance improvisation.

Considerations

Dance Improvisation for Movement Generation

When discussing this purpose, I specifically use the phrase "movement generation" for several reasons. First, the word "movement" broadens the conversation to a larger and more inclusive context. As will be discussed in Chapter 14, there are many forms of dance improvisation, and each is based in the various areas in which they are being explored. Additionally, using the word "movement" continues our concept of the Human Movement Buffet, and that the ultimate goal of any dance improvisation is to broaden the samples of this buffet from which we can draw.

It is also worth noting at this time that the idea of "movement generation" exists itself within two sub categories:

(1) Movement generation for the purpose of enhancing vocabulary and skill.
(2) Movement generation for the purpose of exploration of ideas and concepts in a manner that is unfamiliar to the movement creator (i.e. choreographer/dance maker/s).

Perhaps the easiest entry point for this conversation is the idea of movement generation for the purpose of enhancing vocabulary and/or skill. This is the place where many of us have been exposed to dance improvisation, and, perhaps, the place in which we feel most comfortable. Many practitioners of dance improvisation understand that dance improvisation is a great way to expand one's own movement vocabulary, challenge oneself with new ways of moving/creating, and introducing young dancers to a wider array of movement styles. Similarly, many choreographers also understand the benefits of using dance improvisation within their rehearsal process.

Similar to the benefits/desires of personal movement generation for the purpose of enhancing vocabulary and skill, dance improvisation within the choreographic and rehearsal process can be used for the purpose of exploring ideas/

concepts (both ephemeral and physical) in a manner that is unfamiliar to the dance/movement maker. Yes, dance improvisation in this context can certainly assist a choreographer with items such as choreographer's block, a desire to break from their traditional movement choices, and/or explore ways in which the dancers themselves can contribute to the work. Allowing dancers to contribute to the actual movement creation not only allows alternative voices into the mix, but is also creates space for conversations and expanded movement ideas surrounding the choreographic work. This ultimately reduces the burden placed upon the choreographer to be the sole expert in the space.

Both purposes (movement generation for the purpose of enhancing vocabulary and skill, and movement generation for the purpose of exploration of ideas and concepts in a manner that is unfamiliar to movement creator) are, as mentioned, where most individuals have been exposed to dance improvisation. However, there are two more purposes that need to be discussed: both for their importance, as well as for identifying their similarities and differences.

Dance Improvisation in a Performance

Many young dancers have already been exposed to this second purpose of dance improvisation whether they know it or not. How many times have you heard (or perhaps even said) something to the idea of, "okay, for the next 16 counts you will all do something you want, and then come back together for the unison section." While a crude example of Dance Improvisation within a Performance, this is, in fact, an example.

The idea that improvisation can be used within a codified and cleaned dance piece is nothing new, but perhaps the manner in which we use/address it can be. As mentioned, while instructing dancers to "do something they want for the next 16 counts" is an example of Dance Improvisation within a Performance, it abandons all of the preceding rules we have discussed in this book: chiefly, the idea that there is no right or wrong, but sometimes. there is a better choice. Yes, improvisation can be "whatever a person wants," but as discussed in Chapter 1, this negates the rich and deep contributions that dance improvisation has to offer. Above all, it completely disaffirms the idea of context: this being that anything done outside of a given setting/situation is, at best, jarring, and, at worst, harmful.

Therefore, when inserting dance improvisation within a performance/dance piece, I always suggest taking into account the context of the dance work:

What is the movement vocabulary that already exists?
What is the emotional/conceptual state in which the piece is set?
What is the message (if any) that is being conveyed?
What are the musical cues that accompany this section of improvisation?
What is the ultimate goal for this section being improvised?

When viewing Dance Improvisation in a Performance through the lens of these questions, one can see that dance improvisation can be a powerful tool for enhancing a dance work, as well as providing space for spontaneous pleasantries of the performers. In fact, this type of improvisation, along with its many benefits, already exists in specific dance forms and other artistic forms. Improvisation in jazz music has always been a foundation on which both prescribed performance and spontaneous creation have occurred. We also see this type of improvisation in dance forms such as Hip Hop (the cipher), vernacular jazz dance, and tap dance.

In all of these forms, improvisation occurring within a performance setting always takes into account the context of the moment (be it in time signature, key signature, tempo, groove, etc.) Equally as important, improvisation in these settings also maintains a sense of self-awareness: always knowing its place within the group. Therefore, *improvisation within a performance setting rarely, if ever, is simply about what the improviser desires solely.*

Dance Improvisation as Performance

The final purpose of dance improvisation is Dance Improvisation as Performance. I am referring to a fully realized dance/movement work that has no set structure/ choreography, and is improvised from beginning to end. This, of any of the purposes, is where I tend to see students express both fear and apprehension. It is this specific form of improvisation that seems to be the most mysterious, hard to describe and ephemeral. When done poorly it can feel like watching a bad B-movie, and when done well it can appear as though anyone can do it. After all, aren't the performers just "making stuff up as they go along."

Rule #7 – The Hardest Part Isn't Knowing When to Start

What those of us who practice and teach dance improvisation are very aware of is that it takes years of training and skill in order to make something extremely hard look very easy. Remember, I said at the beginning of this book, dance improvisation is a technique, and like all other dance techniques *its purpose is to provide training so that its practitioners can accomplish difficult tasks with ease.*

Aside from the aforementioned items that can make Dance Improvisation as a Performance challenging, one item above all makes it the scariest for students: How do I begin? The beautiful answer is you begin with Rule # 2 (Start with What You Know), and the more training you have, the more of what you know increases.

Try

Exercise #1: Introduction to Group Improvisation

This is the first time you will begin to introduce your students to improvising as an entire class. At this point it is highly recommended that you take time to review the previous six rules of improvisation. Take time to discuss all that has been discovered thus far, what questions may still be lingering, and, ideally, see if all of the students are able to repeat the rules from memory. While this may sound cultish (hang in there, I promised you from the beginning I would demystify improvisation), the real purpose behind memorizing the rules is to ensure that they are always at the forefront of the students minds. Most importantly, as we begin to introduce large group improvisation we want to ensure that Rule #1 and Rule #5 are ever present in our students' minds.

At this time, you have two options as they pertain to getting your students started:

(1) The sink or swim method.
(2) The guided method.

While the sink or swim method (i.e. instructing your students to begin without guidance) can be effective in reminding the students how much more there is to learn, I have found this method to be the very reason many students have such horrid memories of dance improvisation.

Therefore, I recommend the guided method. Not only does this method provide a more concrete and controlled entry point into the practice of large group dance improvisation, but it also allows you and your students to physically revisit the exercises completed thus far as a means of familiarity. With all of this stated, let us begin.

Entry Point #1 – Walking Exercise

As discussed earlier in this book, I love this exercise for its simplicity and reflection of the **Cycle of Improvisation.** Additionally, it is a simple way to ensure that the students' attention is in the space and on each other. Lastly, by beginning with this exercise you/the students are using the *10 Rules of Imposition: Plus 1* as a means of problem solving. In other words, you are having them follow Rule # 3 (Start with What You Know) and Rule #4 (When in Doubt, Go Back to the Beginning).

By introducing this particular exercise as an entry point into a large group improvisation, you are assisting your students in discovering that the exercises they performed (i.e. the "technique" portion of the class) are, in fact, the very things they can/should use in order to accomplish improvisation.

Instruct your students to begin walking around the room.

- As before, instruct them to start and stop walking as they desire.
- After some time has passed, instruct half of the students participating to stop walking and to simply stand still. These students will remain in the space, but will watch and observe as the remainder of the students continue on.
- Instruct the observing students to take a mental note of when they see something in the space around them that catches their attention. You will ask them to share their findings later on in the class.

Instruct the students who are still walking to now transition to "move through the space, but no two ways the same."

- As with walking, these students can, at their own discretion, decide to pause their locomotive movement and then start again. This allows the moving students to continue for longer by giving them periods of rest.
- Allow the students who are moving through space to continue for some time before instructing them to find an ending place.
- Once these students have found a place to settle and stand, instruct the students who were observing to begin walking again.

- After allowing them to walk for some time, instruct them to move through the space no two ways the same.
- Remember to instruct the standing students to observe what is going on around them, taking mental notes of when something interesting catches their eye.

After some time has passed, instruct the moving students to find a place to settle/end their movement. Once all students have stopped, gather them in a circle to discuss. Consider the following questions:

- As an observer, what moments caught your attention? Why do you think those moments stood out to you?
- As a mover, what other ideas (if any) came to mind as you were moving through space? Did you have any other impulses? If so, what were they? Did you follow them? Why not?
- How could this exercise lead you further into a full dance improvisation? What other tools do you have that you could incorporate?

Repeat this exercise as many times as you desire, or feel free to mix it up with the other entry exercise entry points discussed.

Entry Point #2 – Mirror Exercise

I enjoy this exercise as an entry point because it starts from a place of sharing, since the students will be improvising with more than one person.

As a preparation for entry into large group improvisations, as well as fuller/lengthier improvisations, this exercise provides a springboard for expansion and growth.

As with the original Mirror Exercise, have your students split themselves into pairs, and appoint a Person A and a Person B.

- For simplicity sake, have Person A begin the exercise and have Person B follow. However, unlike the previous execution of this exercise, the students can begin to transfer between the leader and the follower fairly quickly. This shouldn't be too difficult since the students will have practiced this exercise many times by this point in the curriculum.
- As the students continue to mirror one another in their pairs, you may now instruct them to look at other pairs for inspiration. Person A, for example,

may decide to start mirroring another person from a different pair. At this point Person B may choose to continue to follow Person A, or they may choose to also mirror a different pair.

- At first instruct each student to remain within proximity to their original pair, but they may continually bounce between the idea of following their partner or following someone from a different pair.

Once this process has transpired for a while, instruct the students to continue, but they may choose to physically leave their original pair in order to join/mirror a different person.

- First instruct the students that if a new person joins your pair, one of the two of them must leave the pair and join a different group in order to maintain two people in physical proximity at any given time. This of course will start a chain reaction throughout the space/class, forcing the students to make decisions (i.e. improvise/follow their impulse) of when to leave and when to join a group.

- This constant state of mirroring and decision making will prepare your students for later improvisations where multiple stimuli and impulses are continuously affecting them, and they will have to make split-second decisions on which impulses/stimuli to act upon and which ones to ignore.

Once this exercise has transpired for some time, instruct the students to "bring it to a close" or "find an ending."

- Personally, I prefer to state "find an ending," at which point I slowly countdown from the number 10. I have found that this method allows the students the mental time needed to slowly process that an ending must be found, and encourages them to stay in motion rather than stopping abruptly. This will be helpful in later dance improvisations where the goal is to find a collective ending.

Once an ending has been found, gather the students in your discussion circle.' Consider asking your students the following questions:

- How was this entry point different from the walking entry point? Do you have a preference for one or the other? Why? Why not?

Rule #7 – The Hardest Part Isn't Knowing When to Start

- What led to your impulse to mirror someone from a different pair? Was this choice easy to make? Was it easier to make when you had to move to the new pair, knowing someone would have to leave in order for you join? Did knowing this sometimes affect whether, or not, you chose to leave?
- What led you to decide to leave your pair when someone else joined? Was it difficult at first? Why? Why not? Did it become easier after having to move several times?
- How could we combine the walking exercise with this exercise? How could this lead us into larger and lengthier dance improvisations?
- What additional skills do you feel we still need to gain in order to be more comfortable with starting a dance improvisation from scratch?

Following these discussions, have the students repeat the exercise.

- Remind them of the information and epiphanies made during discussion, and that this new information should inform them as they repeat the exercise.

Repeat this exercise as many times as necessary until you feel your students are able to make decisions and adaptations with little to no hesitation.

Entry Point #3 – Group Mirroring Exercise

I recommend this exercise after performing the mirroring exercise due to its similarity.

As mentioned with the mirroring exercise, this exercise creates an environment where multiple stimuli and impulses are continuously affecting the students, and they are forced to make split-second decisions on which impulses/stimuli to act upon and which ones to ignore. However, unlike the mirror exercise, this exercise exponentially increases the number of stimuli.

Similar to the original group mirroring exercise, have your students split up into groups of 3 or 4, forming either a triangle or diamond pattern.

- Instruct the students to begin the exercise from its most advanced stage (if you need a refresher revisit Chapter 6).
- Allow the original version of this exercise to continue until you feel like the students have regained their confidence performing this exercise.

Now, similar to the partner mirror exercise, instruct the students that they may choose to continue to mirror the leader of their group, or they may choose to begin to mirror another group.

- As with the partner mirroring exercise, if a student decides to mirror another group they must still remain within the pattern of their established group. They may choose to bounce between mirroring other groups and their own group, as well as choosing to be the leader of their group (i.e. mirroring no one).
- As an added twist, students may also now decide to follow anyone in their own group, even if that person is not the appointed leader.

After this exercise has transpired for some time, instruct the students to find an ending. Before moving on to the next iteration of this exercise, it may be worth pausing here to circle and discuss what the students experienced.

Consider asking your students the following questions:

- What did you experience?
- Did you ever feel lost? Why? Why not?
- Did you ever find yourself alone in your movement? How did that make you feel? What was your impulse when you discovered this?
- Did you ever become overwhelmed in this exercise? What choices did/could you make to focus back in?
- How did physical proximity affect your ability to mirror someone? Did this affect your impulse on who to follow?

Following these discussions, have your students repeat the exercise again.

- Remind them of the information and epiphanies made during discussion, and that this new information should inform them as they repeat the exercise.
- Repeat this exercise as many times as necessary until you feel your students are able to make decisions and adaptations with ease and confidence.
- Once you feel your students have reached this point, it is time for the next iteration of this exercise.

The next iteration of this exercise follows the same structure as Entry Point #2.

Rule #7 – The Hardest Part Isn't Knowing When to Start

- Students can now make the decision to leave their original group in order to join a different group.
- Similarly, when a new person joins a group, one of the group members must make a choice to leave the group in order to maintain the same number of individuals in the pattern.
- Allow this variation of the exercise to continue to for some time before instructing the students to find an ending. Once again, consider circling up for discussion.

Consider posing the following questions:

- How was this iteration different from the previous version?
- What opportunities were discovered with this newest version?
- What new challenges presented themselves?
- How did physical proximity affect your ability to mirror someone? Did this affect your impulse on who to follow?

Following these discussions, have your students repeat the exercise again.

- Remind them of the information and epiphanies made during discussion, and that this new information should inform them as they repeat the exercise.
- Repeat this exercise as many times as necessary until you feel your students are confident and comfortable.
- Once you feel your students have reached this point, it is time for the final iteration of this exercise.

The final iteration of this exercise allows your students the freedom now to stay in their group, even if a new person joins. In other words, there is no limitation on how big or small a group can get.

- Additionally, students now have permission to break off from a group and begin to improvise on their own with the sole intent of perhaps staring a new group.
- This final version begins to introduce the students to the idea of playing between group improvisation and solo improvisation, two distinct explorations that have, as of yet, not occurred simultaneously.

Rule #7 – The Hardest Part Isn't Knowing When to Start

- After the exercise continues for quite some time, instruct the students to find an ending. However, this time the ending must be accomplished by everyone moving in unison. This is a final twist and surprise to this exercise.

As always, once an ending is found, circle up for discussion and pose the following questions:

- How was this iteration different than the previous version?
- What opportunities were discovered with this newest version?
- What new challenges presented themselves?
- What new discoveries did you make?
- If you started your own new group, what impulse led to this decision? What would you have done if no one had joined you?
- Was it difficult to find an ending where everyone was moving in unison? Why or Why not?
- How could we combine the walking exercise and the partner mirror exercise with this exercise? How could this lead us into larger and lengthier dance improvisations?
- What other exercises could we pull from in order to add more varieties to this exercise?
- What additional skills do you feel we still need to gain in order to be more comfortable with staring a dance improvisation from scratch?

Following these discussions, have your students repeat the exercise again. Remind them of the information and epiphanies made during discussion, and that this new information should inform them as they repeat the exercise. Repeat this exercise as many times as necessary.

Entry Point #4 – Negative Space Exercise

This entry point very much follows the same beginning and progression as Entry Point #2. However, unlike that entry point, this time the students will jump directly to joining another pair if/when they feel the impulse. This is because we are currently working with proximal negative space, and therefore the students must be proximal to one another in order to accomplish the task at hand.

Rule #7 – The Hardest Part Isn't Knowing When to Start

- Similar to Entry Point #2, one student in the pair must chose to leave their pair if a new student joins.
- After some time instruct the class to find an ending.
- You will want to gather around for discussion again, and you may use any of the questions listed in the previous exercises, or you may choose to introduce new questions based on what you observed your students both struggling with and succeeding in.
- After your discussion is completed, have your students repeat the exercise as many times as necessary before moving on to the next progression.

The second progression of this exercise follows the second and third iteration of Entry Point #3.

- As with those two iterations, be sure to allow plenty of time for exploration and development before instructing the students to find an ending.
- Also be sure to hold discussions between each iteration, as well as repeating each iteration several times before moving onto the next.
- Lastly, be sure to take a moment to remind your students of Rule #1 (*Sometimes There is a Better Choice*), and Rule #5 (*The Moment You Check Out Someone Gets Hurt*). There will be many more bodies in space now, and all within proximal distance of one another.
- Particularly, in the third iteration of this exercise there is no maximum or minimum to the number of individuals in a group working within the negative space of one another, and therefore the chance for physical injury is increased.
- Lastly, rather than the end goal of unison movement from the previous entry point, the goal now is to have every student exploring the negative space of every other student. Ultimately in order to find an ending, the class as a whole must settle on a "feeling" that now is the time to slow the improvisation down and end in a manner that we all agree.

Entry Point #5 – Touch Exercise.

This entry point is the most advanced entry point, and therefore should not be attempted until all previous entry points have been mastered.

- This is a good time to once again stress our safety rules of Rule #1 (*Sometimes There is a Better Choice*), and Rule #5 (*The Moment You Check Out Someone Gets Hurt*).

Rule #7 – The Hardest Part Isn't Knowing When to Start

- Additionally, you will need to remind the students that this is not contact improvisation, and therefore there should be no weight sharing, counter balancing, or lifting.
- At this point in the curriculum touch is used only to supply a tactile stimulation point, and therefore students should stick only with the options to either move toward or away from the touch, or pause when being touched.
- It is always good practice to repeat this exercise in its original iteration to ensure students are comfortable and remember the rules of engagement.

This exercise follows the exact progression and interactions as Entry Point #4. Again, after each iteration is completed be sure to stop, circle up, and lead a discussion. Feel free to use any of the questions provided in this chapter or create your own based on what you see during the exercise. Similar to the ending of Entry Point #4, an ending for this final iteration entails the class as a whole finding an unspoken and non-predetermined conclusion this is mutually agreed upon.

Notes

Rule #8 – Everything You Need Exists in the World around You

Introduction

You may have noticed that up until this point, we have not discussed items such as music, lighting, mood, atmosphere, and space/location. While all of these items can, and likely will, affect the manner and approach to dance improvisation, until this point in the curriculum I have intentionally left them out of the conversation.

By this point in the curriculum, your students should begin to have a firm grasp on their movement habits, new found approach for inspiration, and working within a larger group setting. In Chapter 4, I discussed the various types of impulses, their definitions, and how to tap into each of them. I also stated that a large portion of a young improviser's journey begins with understanding and addressing Non-Biological Internal Impulses: those impulses students think they control, but, in all actuality, do not. I also promised that we would, at a later time, address **Non-Biological External Impulses**. Now is that time.

Context

Let me first begin with the reasons why I discourage teachers from using music (specifically) until this point in the curriculum. Dancers, more so than perhaps any other human group, with perhaps the exception of musicians, have spent their entire training career learning to lean on music as the driving force for their creativity, physical execution, and direction. Music is, in a very real sense, the force by which many dancers determine their movement creativity.

While this may seem like an over exaggeration, when we consider that many (if not most) dance classes in the United States (and perhaps globally) do not "officially begin" until the music starts, it becomes clear why music is

DOI: 10.4324/9781003387084-11

such a driving force in a dancer's world. To drive this point home even further, recall the number of times your students have expressed feeling uneasy, weird, or silly when they are asked to execute any movement, even walking, without musical accompaniment. Music, for one reason or another, dictates a dancer's environment, and silence, in contrast, is to be avoided at all costs. It is precisely because of these reasons (and many more) that I do not allow music in dance improvisation until this point. Simply put, *music is yet another habit that our dancers cannot control* – and therefore is now an addiction.

If our goal is to create thinking-creative movement artists, then we must, and I again repeat MUST, start with movement. This being said, do not misunderstand me regarding my thoughts on music alone. Music can be a wonderful source of inspiration and impulse once an improviser has complete control over his/her/their own inherent movement and creative biases. I myself have been an active musician (playing everything from the French horn to the didgeridoo) since the fifth grade. However, I would argue that many young dancers in training in the United State do not have a full grasp of the complexities of music. Very few young dancers know how to read sheet music, and most don't know how to count music outside of the standard 4/4 and 4/8 time signatures.

Perhaps even more disheartening is that many young dancers don't even know how to listen to music. They have spent their days listening to compressed digital versions of music (if you didn't know, digital music does not actually contain all of the sounds available in a recording), and they generally multitask while listening to music. Thus, their attention is not dedicated to the nuances, depth, textures, and feelings that music produces. Rather, they listen to merely the words and tempos of a song.

This behavior has now led to several generations of young movers who view sounds and music not as a source of infinite inspiration, but rather as mere backdrops to daily living. To combat this, I would like to propose that we first dive into the richness of music before addressing specific ways in which we can train our students how to use music as a **Non-Biological External Impulse.**

Considerations

To being, let me first break down the idea of "music" into two separate categories:

A. Assorted Auditory Sounds.
B. Structured Auditory Phrases.

Rule #8 – Everything You Need Exists in the World around You

I think these distinctions are important because when I use the word "music," many individuals suddenly conjure some sort of soundscape. However, it is easy to assume that no two individuals conjure the same soundscape, and thus, what is music to one person may be noise to another.

The term music, like touch, is burdened with cultural, generational, and historical baggage, and is therefore difficult to remove personal feelings, emotions, ideas and memories associated with any one specific style or genre of music. This therefore inherently affects both how we hear music, and how that music may, or may not, inspire us to move.

As a means of assisting this conversation, Figure 10.1 demonstrates how I tend to break down music into subcategories:

My guess is that when I say "music," your mind goes directly to the far, bottom right box (Metered Soundscape). This box contains what many people typically think of when given the term music. This box encompasses everything from Beethoven, to rap, to Carnatic music, to Samba; and everything in between. However, when viewing this chart we can see that music in all its forms covers a vast spectrum of sounds, noises, and melodies:

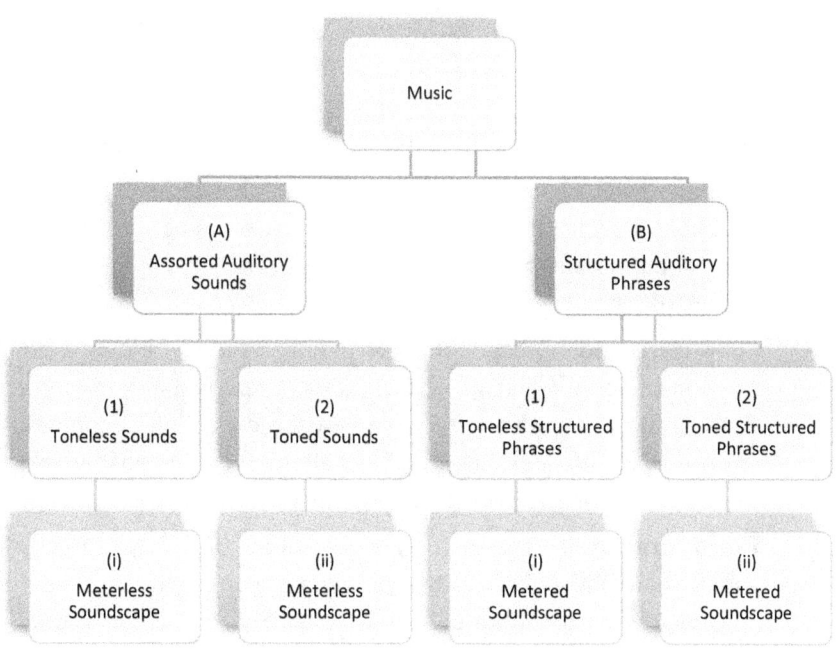

Figure 10.1 Music Category Chart

A. **Assorted Auditory Sounds (A)** encompasses all sounds that occur in a non-rhythmic/non-metered manner. We might call this category chaos or random sounds.
   Toneless (A.1) and **Toned Sounds (A.2).**
   1. **Toneless Sounds (A.1)** – All sounds that do not have a distinct tone/note associated with them: scratching, scraping, breaking, clapping, stomping, slapping, breathing, hissing, etc.), but do not contain an identifiable rhythm Your students have already been exposed to these sounds as a basis for impulse via Exercise #3 in Chapter 4.
      i. **Meterless Soundscape (A.1.i)** – Singular sounds and/or a collection of sounds that make up a larger experiential auditory landscape (e.g. soundscapes that consist of a collection of non-descript noises.)
   2. **Toned Sounds (A.2)** – All sounds that have an identifiable tone/note associated with them.
      ii. **Meterless Soundscape (A.2.ii)** – Singular sounds and/or a collection of sounds that make up a larger experiential auditory landscape, but do not contain an identifiable rhythm (e.g. soundscapes played at a specified hertz for rest and/or relaxation)
B. **Structured Auditory Phrases (B)** encompasses any sound/s that have an identifiable pattern. This category contains much of what the Western Hemisphere considered music.
   Toneless Structured Phrases (B.1) and **Toned Structured Phrases (B.2)**
   1. **Toneless Structured Phrases (B.1)** - All sounds that do not have a distinct tone/note associated with them: scratching, scraping, breaking, clapping, stomping, slapping, breathing, hissing, etc.), and are arranged in a structured/repeated/predictable phrase.
      i. **Metered Soundscape (B.2.i)** – Singular sounds and/or a collection of sounds that make up a larger experiential auditory landscape (e.g. soundscapes that consist of a collection of non-descript noises.) with a <u>distinguishable</u> pattern (i.e. identifiable rhythm, tempo and/or times signatures).
   2. **Toned Structured Phrases (B.2)** – All sounds that have an identifiable tone/note associated with them, and are arranged in a structured/repeated/predictable phrase.
      ii. **Metered Soundscape (B.2.ii)** – Singular sounds and/or a collection of sounds that make up a larger experiential auditory landscape

(e.g. our standard understanding of music) with a <u>distinguishable</u> pattern (i.e. identifiable rhythm, tempo and/or times signatures).

I could dive into a deeper investigation of music theory, the science of wave lengths, and how sound vibrations affect our physical bodies, but for the sake of time and brevity let's simply settle on the fact that music and sound are two deeply complex items of which many (if not most) young dancers have generally merely scratched the surface.

Perhaps even more importantly, let's settle on the fact that music, as the general young dancer in training experiences it, is a small portion of the greater experience that sound and music have to offer. I encourage you to explore all of the categories and subcategories in the supplied chart, but for now let us move onto inspirations/impulses that some, and sometimes all, of the categories in the chart supply us with. As a useful tip, from here on out I will use the words *music* and *sound* interchangeably. This is meant to aid you in embracing the idea that the two need not be separate.

Impulses and Inspiration in Music

When listening to sound, there are five key indicators that I pay close attention to. These indicators serve as sources for inspiration and impulse, allowing me to further investigate and experience the music. These indicators are **Time, Texture, Energy/Dynamics, Sensation/Feeling,** and **Shape**. Each helps to shape my listening experience as well as what ultimately inspires me.

The following is a brief description of each:

- **Time** deals with both tempo and experienced time. Tempo can be both speed and time signature, while experienced time is the actual passage of time I feel while listening.
- **Texture** addresses various experiences of the music. Does the music feel heavy, or does it feel light? Does it feel smooth, or does it feel coarse? Does it feel pointed, or does it feel soft?
- **Energy/Dynamic** address both the motion of the music, as well as the actual dynamics. By motion I am referring to the directional energy one feels when hearing the sound. Does it have a forward or backward motion? If it is a forward motion, is it a jog or a sprint? Dynamics, on the other hand, refers to the various levels of volume. Is it loud or soft? Does it increase in volume, or decrease?

- **Sensation/Feeling** deals with the actual emotional state one experiences when hearing the music. This in turn can influence the way in which one moves as an improviser.
- **Shape** addresses the form of the music. Is there an arc to the sound? Is it round or square? Is it angular or curved? Does it resolve, or does it merely disperse?

These five principles of sound, while not fully complete, are a beginning step toward assisting our students with understanding how sound can influence their movement choices. Additionally, these principles allow our students to tap deeper into their imaginations and newly developed movement vocabulary by encouraging them to draw closer to the Non-Biological External Impulses given. Finally, understanding these principles empowers our students by giving them the tools and methods by which they themselves can determine whether or not they choose to follow the supplied impulse. Overall their listening and physical reacting are influenced by a much richer experience than simply reacting to the words or tempos of the music.

Additional External Impulses and Inspiration

While music is certainly a potent and powerful Non-Biological External Impulse, I would be remiss to not mention and discuss the various additional Non-Biological External Impulses. Quite simply, we need to investigate the five senses used by our bodies:

(1) Touch
(2) Taste
(3) Smell
(4) Hearing
(5) Sight.

While we have already discussed hearing, and I certainly would not necessarily suggest investigating taste or smell during a dance improvisation class, touch and sight are certainly items worth discussing. This being said, taste and smell certainly can be used based on the students' experiences outside the class.

Visual Stimuli

Beginning first with sight, it is imperative to understand that this sense, above all others, is many dancers' most prominent sense. Dancers use their sight to replicate movement demonstrated by a teacher and/or choreographer almost on a daily basis. They use their sight to check themselves in the mirror (sometimes too much) in order to find the correct shape and/or placement of a position. This is of no surprise since dancers are, after all, humans, and human beings eyes are located on the front of the face, rather than the sides of the face like most other animals.

Therefore, much of how we experience the world is through our eyes. Yet, I would argue that, much like music, we rarely visually experience the world in all its depth and richness. Rather, we generally relegate the visual world to a blurry background that accompanies our daily living, ignoring the various wonders and signs it offers us. Therefore, if we are to aid out students in becoming creative beings we must introduce them to the world in which they live; as opposed to the world in which they have lived.

Much like music, I tend to break visual/sight into five usable inspirations/indicators: **Color, Shape, Texture, Movement,** and **Size/Scale**. The following is a brief description of each:

- **Color** addresses both the actual color of an item, as well as how that color informs my emotions. This can be a tricky area as color has various cultural, emotional, historical, and societal meanings, all of which can then influence how an individual experiences the actual color. Therefore, I highly encourage you to explore both the general idea of any specific color with your students, as well as various interpretations of that color.
- **Shape** refers to the specific silhouette of an object/objects. This is not the assigned feeling of the shape, but rather the actual name and title given (i.e. square, circle, triangle, hexagon, parallelogram, etc.). A simple impulse would be to try and replicate the assigned shape name with one's body. However, one could also address the items that make up the shape (i.e. line, arc, point, etc.).
- **Texture** addresses what the object does, or may, feel like. Is it rough or smooth? Is it warm or cold? Is it fine or jagged? All of these can be used as impulses for movement exploration.
- **Movement** acknowledges that not all items viewed are stationary. Many, in fact, move through space. Rather than simply settle with the idea that an

object is in motion, I also suggest investigating how and in what manner it moves. Does it move fast or slow? Does it walk or roll? Is it graceful or lumbering? All of these finer points create a much richer movement impulse, and therefore require a larger movement vocabulary.

- **Size and Scale** refer to both the height of the object, as well as the imaginable weight and mass. Both of these items are relative based on context (a skyscraper is huge to you and I, but miniature to a giant), and therefore be sure, like the idea of movement, to go deeper into exploration.

It is now easier to understand that the visual word is full of multifaceted impulses and inspirations. We must merely take the time to fully investigate each area. Also, as with sound, by giving our students the tools and methods by which to fully investigate the visual world, we free them of the same, mundane movement choices they make based on what they see. We can now aid them in fully dissecting the visual world in various bite-sized stimuli that will grow and mature their movement choices.

Tactile Stimuli

Touch is the final Non-Biological External Impulse to be discussed. While touch has already been explored in this book, the main purpose of our earlier exploration was to learn how to touch and be touched without indication. However, what has not been explored is the many ways in which touch can supply an improviser with inspiration on how to move and when to move.

It is ironic that despite the skin being the largest organ of the human body, we spend so little time as dancers exploring the many ways in which this super sensor can inform our creative side. When investigating touch I spend my time focusing on three principle indicators as a means of movement generation: **Texture, Temperature,** and **Movement**.[1] Texture and Temperature are fairly self-explanatory, but Movement is perhaps less known to young improvisers.

Without venturing into the realm of Contact Improvisation (a version of improvisation addressed in Chapter 14), it is helpful to simply think of movement as the location of an object and the direction of its movement as indicated by touch. In other words, is this person/object to the side of me, the back of me, or the front of me, and/or is this person/object in motion? If so, what direction

Rule #8 – Everything You Need Exists in the World around You

are they headed? While the purpose of this understanding is not to interact with the object/individual based on these indicators (again this leads into Contact Improvisation), they can be used as sources of inspiration requiring some sort of physical response/reaction.

Now that we have a better understanding of the various ways in which "Everything We Need Exists in the World Around Us," let us now begin exploring these indicators with our students.

Try

Exercise #1: Listening to Music, Picking an Indicator, Explore the Indicator

You may start this exercise with the class as a whole, but eventually you will want to separate the class into smaller groups. However, starting with the class as whole will allow for greater conversation and a wider variety of opinions.

Begin by writing the various sound indicators on small pieces of paper and place them into a bag, hat, or large bowl.

- Be sure to delineate which specific aspect of an indicator you desire (i.e. Time – tempo, or Time – experienced time).
- Have a student reach into the bag and draw out a piece of paper.
- You or the student may read aloud what is on the piece of paper.

Now have your students spread out throughout the space (ensure there is room for each of them to move), and turn on a piece of sound/music.

- Instruct your students to listen to the sound first, reminding them that they are listening for the specific sound indicator that was pulled out from the bag.
- As the students feel inspired they may now begin to move in a manner that reflects their interpretation of the sound via the lens of the chosen indicator.
- If your space is not large enough for all students to participate, ask half of the students sit around the room and observe those who are moving.
- After some time have the two groups (those moving and those sitting) switch places.

Rule #8 – Everything You Need Exists in the World around You

Repeat this exercise several times.
Several variations of this exercises are as follows:

(1) When the groups switch, the students who were seated, but now are moving, will use the same sound indicator and the same piece of music
(2) When the groups switch, the students who were seated, but now are moving, will use the same sound indicator but a new piece of music
(3) When the groups switch, the students who were seated, but now are moving, will use a new sound indicator but the same piece of music

Any of the above adaptations are correct. Depending on your unique situation, you may find that you stick with one, or you may choose to explore them all. Regardless, once the students have performed this exercise several times, pick a new sound indicator and repeat the exercise.

- Eventually you want to provide a wide variety of music and soundscapes, or perhaps even silence, in order to grow your students' listening capabilities.

As a side note, it is always worth making space for discussion. This can occur between the two groups of students (those seated and those standing) or simply as a whole class.
Consider asking the following questions to spur conversation:

- What differences did you notice in interpretations regarding the sound indicator chosen? Were you inspired by any of these different interpretations?
- What soundscapes did you find it easy to find inspiration in? Why? What specific sound indicators stood out to you?
- What soundscapes did you find it challenging to find inspiration in? Why? What specific sound indicators could you use in order to overcome this difficulty?
- What sound indicators did you find it easy to hear and find inspiration in? Why?
- What sound indicators did you find it difficult to hear and find inspiration in? Why?

As you continue this exercise you will eventually want to expand the number of sound indicators that students simultaneously explore. I recommend starting small by first pulling only two sound indicators out of the bag. Giving your students full access to any and all sound indicators too quickly will result in

1. your students either being overwhelmed by the choices and thus becoming paralyzed to make a decision, or
2. your students being overwhelmed by the amount of choices and therefore returning simply to their previous biases.

Eventually you can open as many sound indicators to your students as you/they desire; but, as always, take is slow. *Remember, the destination is the journey.*

Exercise #2: Clapping Exercise, but with Sounds

For a refresher on the clapping exercise, revisit Exercise #3 in Chapter 4. However, as a quick reminder you will have your students split themselves into smaller groups and have each group sit in their own small circle.

- Ask one person from each group for a volunteer to step into and stand the middle of their circle.
- The task is simple: the person in the middle of each group will make a shape with their body each time she/he/they hears a member of their group clap.
- If multiple claps occur simultaneously (let's say three claps), then the person in the middle must do three rapid shapes.
- You may want to perform a full round of this exercise before moving on to this newest version.

The newer version of this exercise will ask the students who are sitting to now make a sound, rather than simply clap.

- As before, the person in the middle will react to the sound.
- However, this time they must take into account the five music/sound principles (Time, Texture, Energy/Dynamics, Sensation/Feeling, and Shape) when choosing their shape.
- You will want to encourage the seated students to give the person in the center of the circle more time between sounds, since the mover in the center of the circle must now take into account multiple indicators.

Rule #8 – Everything You Need Exists in the World around You

There are several ways to adapt and/or expand on this exercise:

(1) Have the person in the center of the circle focus on only one of the five principles.
(2) Give the person in the center freedom to choose which singular principle they will react to. This may change with each new sound.
   a. As an expansion to this specific version, you may also make a game out of if by having the students who are seated guess which sound principle the person in the center was reacting to.
(3) Give the person in the center the freedom to choose multiple music principles to incorporate.
   a. As an expansion to this specific exercise, you may also make a game out of if by having the students who are seated guess which principle/s the person in the center was reacting to.
(4) Instruct the students sitting to create a structured pattern of sounds, thus causing the person in the center to improvise in a rhythmic pattern.
(5) Instruct the students sitting to "sing" notes rather than making sounds, thus giving the person in the center an additional source of inspiration.
(6) Instruct the students sitting to switch between Toneless-Meterless sounds, and Toned-Metered sounds.

Exercise #3: Return to the Object Game

As a quick reminder I recommend you review Exercise #2 from Chapter 4.

- During that original exercise the students were asked to sit in a circle around the room.
- In the middle of the circle you placed an object.
- Students were then instructed to come to the center of the circle (one at a time) and use the object in any manner other than that of the object's intended purpose.

For this newer version you will instruct your students to come to the center of the circle and briefly improvise based on any of the five **Visual Stimuli** (Color, Shape, Texture, Movement, and Size/Scale) discussed in this chapter.

Rule #8 – Everything You Need Exists in the World around You

- Instruct the students to only pick one visual indicator to focus on.
- To make the game feel more engaging, the students who are seated will guess which visual indicator the student improvising used as their inspiration.
- Be sure to leave time later on in the class for discussion regarding choices made by each improviser.
- As with the original version of this exercise, I suggest starting with larger objects (perhaps even the very same ones you used in Chapter 4) and work your way to smaller objects.

A few additional items to consider:

(1) Starting with the first object, once the first student is completed with their improvisation, and perhaps discussion has occurred, leave the same object at the center of the circle. Each consecutive student must pick a different visual indicator until all five indicators have been used.

(2) Once all five indicators have been used on the same object, you may now either:

   a. keep the same object in the center, but now allow students to focus on more than one indicator, or

   b. swap out objects at the center of the circle and repeat the same process again.

Exercise #4: Moving Away or to the Touch – Expanded

As a reminder, I recommend you review Exercise #3 from Chapter 7. However, as a quick synopsis you will

- Pair your students up and assign each of them a title: Person A and Person B.
- Person A will take the Vitruvian Man position, and Person B will be instructed to begin to touch Person A with the palm of their hand.
- Once touched in/on a location, Person A will move that specific body part toward or away from the touch.
- Allow this exercise to continue for some time (5–7 minutes) before having the students switch roles.

Rule #8 – Everything You Need Exists in the World around You

The new adaptation of this exercise is to have the individual who is moving to/away from the touch to move in such a way that they are reacting to one of the three **Tactile Stimuli** (Texture, Temperature, and Movement). Here are several ways to adapt and expand on this exercise:

(1) Instruct the person being touched to choose only one of the three Tactile Stimuli to focus on during the duration of the exercise.
(2) Instruct the person being touched to choose a different Tactile Stimuli to focus on each time they are touched.
(3) Give the person being touched the freedom to choose from any of the three Tactile Stimuli each time they are touched.
   a. As an expansion to this specific exercise, you may also make a game out of if by instructing the student who is doing the touching to guess which touch principle the person being touched was reacting to. Have them guess and confer with their partner between touches.
(4) Instruct the person doing the touch to choose a Tactile Stimuli they wish to impart, and then touch their partner with this intention.
   a. As an expansion to this specific exercise, you may also make a game out of if by instructing the student who is being touched to guess which Tactile Stimuli the person doing the touching was trying to convey. Have them guess and confer with their partner between touches.

Exercise #5: I Spy

Similar to the game you may have played as a child, this exercise requires your students to look around the studio and "spy" an object. Also similar to the original childhood game, the student who will be demonstrating is required to say "I spy an object that is..." and then proceed to improvise using the five Visual Stimuli (Color, Shape, Texture, Movement, and Size/Scale) discussed in this chapter. The students who are sitting will then guess the object that is being "spied" based on the improvisation and visually searching the room for the object themselves.

A few suggestions before you begin:

(1) I recommend having your students sit in a circle for this exercise. Having students sit on one side of the studio to watch the improviser makes the exercise

feel more "performative," and therefore can reduce the amount of risk-taking that the improvising student may try. Sitting in a circle, on the other hand, allows for the exercise to feel more communal and less high-risk, thus creating space for greater risk-taking. If you so choose, you can certainly break the class into smaller groups, at which point each group would sit in their own circle.

(2) Similar to Exercise #3 in this chapter, you may desire your students to focus on only one visual indicator of the object they spy. While this may make it harder for the students who are guessing the object, it does make it easier for the student who is improvising.

(3) As your students become more comfortable with this game feel free to allow the student improvising to use more Visual Stimuli as inspiration for their movement creation.

(4) Remember to allow time for discussion following the guessing portion among the seated students. *Conversation is the best way for students to learn about physical choices being made by the improviser, and allows the improviser to learn how their physical choices may or may not have connected with the students seated.*

(5) Remind all students that there "is no right or wrong; but sometimes there is a better choice." In this case the better choices are those improvisations that guide the seated students toward the object that is inspiring the improviser.

(6) Be sure to change up your location (indoors and outside, different studios/classrooms, etc.) in order to provide your students with as much variety and richness for visual inspiration as possible.

Citation

1 I also use these three indicators when exploring Taste, as well as Smell.

Notes

Rule #9 – Continual Movement in and of Itself Is Not Necessarily Improvisation

Introduction

Ideally, by this point in the curriculum, your students are feeling comfortable with the idea of improvisation, are excited about each new class, and understand the basics of both individual and group improvisation. If you find that your students are at this point, congratulations! If you find that your students are not at this point, fear not. As I keep reiterating throughout this book, this process (like the training of any dance technique) takes time and is unique to each group of students.

Again, I implore you not to rush this process and push your students to the end of this curriculum simply to say, "We did it." There is a reason we wait for dancers to fully develop before we have them try on their first pair pointe shoes, or before we teach them complicated rhythms in tap dance. The same can be said for dance improvisation. There are portions of this technique that are appropriate for all ages, and there are portions that are only appropriate for mature (both in training and age) students. Trust the process.

If you find that you are now ready to teach this portion of the curriculum, you will probably notice one specific item:

The students want to move…all of the time!

This desire of the students to explore, try, take healthy risks, and play should always be encouraged, and therefore, this chapter must be approached with both ease and caring. The last thing we would ever want to do is make our students regress from all of the work we have accomplished thus far. Therefore,

DOI: 10.4324/9781003387084-12

Rule #9 – Continual Movement in and of Itself Is Not Improvisation

I recommend this chapter and its lessons only for your more mature and developed improvisers.

Context

As the title of this chapter suggests, continual movement, while fun and exciting, is not necessarily improvisation. There is a very distinct difference between movement exploration and improvisation. While these two terms certainly can, and are, intermixed, I would also like to suggest that they each have different outcomes. As discussed in Chapter 9, there are several purposes for dance improvisation:

- Dance Improvisation for Movement Creation
- Dance Improvisation for Performance
- Dance Improvisation within a Performance

Up until this point we have been focusing mainly on Dance Improvisation for Movement Creation. However, we have yet to address the latter two purposes for dance improvisation (i.e. For Performance and Within a Performance). This is where this chapter comes into play.

Dance Improvisation with a Performance

The beginnings of Dance Improvisation within a Performance were addressed (unbeknownst to you the reader) in the last chapter. In that chapter we explored how music/sound, sight, touch, smell, and taste all have indicators/stimuli that we can use to inform and inspire movement creation. As a sum total of all five indicators, I like to use the word "context" (you've been seeing this word throughout the book). In other words, there are times when context must be taken into account when inserting and/or using improvisation.

We see this many times when dance improvisation is used in both tap dance and jazz dance. In tap dance, rhythm and time are particular contexts that an improviser must be aware of and rely on. Within the jazz dance genre, time, aesthetic, vocabulary, and community are just some of the contexts that should be taken into account when improvising. To put it another way, to add a backflip as an improvisational choice during a classical ballet solo, while neither right

Rule #9 – Continual Movement in and of Itself Is Not Improvisation

nor wrong, sacrifices the context (vocabulary, storyline, characterization, etc.) of the performance in pursuit of pure personal expression. Similarly, it would feel out of place (I would imagine) if a dancer started doing fouettés in the middle of a breaking battle.

While little time in this book is dedicated to Dance Improvisation within Performance, all of the tools and training necessary to achieve mastery of this are provided.

- The ability to identify one's own movement biases, and then break free from them is a tool needed for Dance Improvisation within Performance.
- The ability to identify an informed impulse and act on it seamlessly is another necessary tool for Dance Improvisation within Performance.
- The knowledge and skill to be able to fully hear music, see the created world, and feel the environment in depth and richness only adds to one's contextual improvisation within a performance.
- Finally, the ability to improvise within a group setting, using all of the cues given by those around you, is precisely a skill needed in order to improvise within a performance.

All this to be said, the skills trained thus far directly transfer from improvisation as a movement generation practice to the practice of improvising within a performance setting. Perhaps the main difference being the idea of context. That simply comes by practicing improvisation more and within a given context.

Dance Improvisation as a Performance

Dance Improvisation as a Performance is merely a more open understanding of the statement "within a given context." While the context may not be as specific as a tap jam, a House battle, or a classical pas de deux, there is still a context that must now be taken into account: an audience.

This audience is the very reason why I suggest saving this chapter for only your most advanced improvisers. Just like touch and music are encumbered with historic, cultural, and societal baggage, so too is the idea of what an audience is and the expectations a performer must meet when an audience is present. Therefore, I suggest that during this chapter and training we change our language from "audience" to "observers."

Rule #9 – Continual Movement in and of Itself Is Not Improvisation

The word observer has a milder sound, harkening to a state of passivity from the onlooker and a lesser degree of expectation of the improviser. However, despite my attempt to lessen the amount of fear experienced by the improviser/s, there is an existent reality that any observer of dance improvisation brings to a performance: "Is what I am watching interesting?" As I say to my students all of the time, if you are satisfied with singing in the shower, then by all means sing in the shower until the end of your days. *However, if you desire to have others listen to you sing, now you must take into account those individuals' attention spans, desires, realties, and likes/dislikes.*

Dance Improvisation as Performance must address this very same reality. A group of observers brings the expectation that the practice of improvisation is no longer merely about my/our movement exploration. Improvisers must take into account that each impulse, inspiration and movement choice is now subject to the interest, or lack thereof, of the observers. To ensure that a performative dance improvisation remains true to its roots, while also taking into account the desires of the observers, there are several tools that can be implemented in an attempt to make a performance a fuller experience for the observers.

Considerations

Collective and Cohesive Artistic Expression

Not so much a tool as an idea, the concept of a collective and cohesive artistic expression is more of a guiding light than an implementable tool. I would argue that all full (notice I didn't say successful) artistic statements possess this quality. Be it music, dance, theater, visual art, or any other form of artistic expression, a cohesive artistic expression is that item which holds the audience through the inevitable twists and turns of an artistic idea.

In compositional terms we tend to use the word "motif." Whether or not you want to use this word, the idea that an artistic work has a thumbprint (if you will) of its creator/s that expresses an overarching theme/idea is an important factor in sustaining the observers' interest and engagement. How then do we do this in performative dance improvisation?

- Be aware of the need for a cohesive artistic expression.

Rule #9 – Continual Movement in and of Itself Is Not Improvisation

- Find some congruency among several factors. These include, but are not limited to:
  - Texture
  - Timing
  - Shape
  - Tempo
  - Levels
  - Feel/Emotion
  - Energy
  - Sounds/Music Choice

- The improvisers should be relating to/in a movement conversation with one another (i.e. Action and Reaction).

Mapping

Mapping is a tool that is extremely helpful in providing both a possible path and safety rails for an improvisation. Like an actual map, mapping a dance improvisation allows the improvisers to gain a view of the landscape from above, plot possible stops and starts, plan alternate routes, and foresee a possible ending, all the while understanding that adaptation and changes will occur once the realities of the journey commence. Also like a real map/hiking trip, once the group has begun the journey they may collectively decide to abandon the previous plan based on the newly discovered landscape. *Simply put, mapping supplies improvisers with a plan, but not a rule.*

The actually process of mapping is equally fluid. Mapping can be as concrete as the improvisers deciding that at a certain time or cue everyone will move in unison, or to one side of the space, or stop and remain still, or…. whatever specified physical actions they determine. Equally viable, mapping can also be more ephemeral in nature. The improvisers can decide that this improvisation is inspired by, say, a specific color, or object, or sound, or idea. Again, the point of mapping is not so much to stick to the path lest we fall off the planet, but more so provide all improvisers with a collective and cohesive understanding of what the group may wish to present artistically.

Compositional Tools

The tools of composition are a great way to introduce both cohesion and structure. These tools can be used individually, collectively, repeatedly, or as specific touchpoints in a mapped improvisation. Regardless, having an understanding of and the ability to execute the tools of composition can provide the needed structure and guidance a performance improvisation may need.

The following is by no means an exhaustive list of compositional tools, nor are the definitions specific to dance. Rather, the list and its definitions are a general starting point, and can be further explored in both dance improvisation and dance composition.

1. **Canon** – Cannon is a term in which the dancers begin one after another, at regular intervals, successively taking up the same subject or movement phrase of the first dancer. It either ends when the last dancer has completed the entire movement phrase begun by the first dancer, or forms a round (i.e. a canon that repeats itself). A canon may occur in time and/or space.

2. **Unison** – Unison is movement that occurs between two or more dancers in which their actions occur identically and simultaneously in time, space, facing, and energy.

3. **Counterpoint** – Counterpoint is a choreographic element that involves the creation of movement phrases, or stillness, that look very different and move independently from each other, but look harmonious within the theme of a dance when viewed at the same time. Counterpoint can occur both with movement and stillness, as well between two or more dancers. Generally, counterpoint occurs only between two different movement phrases or stillness, but can become more complicated by adding addition phrases or groups of dancers.

4. **Accumulation** – Accumulation is the addition of one or more dancers to an existing or current movement phrase, formation, or space. Accumulation can occur either systematically through a canon, or intermittently, and can join through any of the choreographic elements (unison, counterpoint, etc.)

5. **Subtraction/Dispersion** – Subtraction/ Dispersion is the reduction or dispersal of one or more dancers to an existing or current movement phrase, formation, or space. Subtraction/Dispersion can occur either systematically through cannon or intermittently, and can join through any of the choreographic elements (unison, counterpoint, etc.)

6. **Acceleration** – Acceleration is the gradual or abrupt change (speed up) in tempo, movement phrasing, and/or time. Acceleration in dance can occur either in conjunction with the accompanying music or in juxtaposition to it.
7. **Decelerate/Ritardando** – Decelerate/Ritardando is the gradual or abrupt change (slow down) in tempo, movement phrasing, and/or time. Deceleration in dance can occur either in conjunction with the accompanying music or in juxtaposition to it.
8. **Repetition** – Repetition is the act of replicating a movement phrase, idea, or theme. It is usually performed to bring importance or heightened awareness to a specific idea, or for audience comfort/recognition. In dance improvisation, repetition is easiest executed by either mirroring in repetition, or by executing a short and easily remembered movement phrase multiple times in a row.
9. **Retrograde** – Retrograde is either the literal reversal of movement of a dance phrase, or the reversal of an idea, motif, or theme in dance.
10. **Symmetry** – Symmetry is similar or precise placement between different things. Symmetry can occur in time and/or space.
11. **Asymmetry** – Asymmetry is a lack of (opposing) similar or exact placement between different objects in space.
12. **Suspension/Fermata** – Suspension/Fermata is a pause or gradual slowing of time and/or movement.
13. **Stillness** – Stillness is a state of no movement, which is not equal to lifeless.
14. **Chaos** – Chaos is a state of movement where extreme confusion and disorder occur in time, space, shape, and or motion.
15. **Order** – Order is a systematic approach to movement, where it is deliberately obvious that the movement phrases, ideas, spacing or shapes are meant to be symmetrical in space, time, shape, and/or intent.
16. **Levels** – Levels are various vertical heights at which and in which movement occurs. These levels can be broken into floor work, low level, medium level, and high level.

Calling Scene

The practice of "calling scene" is actually taken from theater training. When an actor or actors complete a scene during their training (i.e. during class time),

Rule #9 – Continual Movement in and of Itself Is Not Improvisation

they will call out "scene." This allows the observers in the space to know that the actor is no longer in character and that the actual scene being presented has concluded. I love this practice for dance improvisation because it allows the improvisers the power to determine an ending. Notice that I said "an ending," and not "the ending." In theory, improvisation could go on forever since, as we discussed in Chapter 1, the Cycle of Improvisation continually feeds on itself. Therefore, dance improvisation at its core has no true ending.

However, understanding that an audience of observers most likely will not stay around forever, it is helpful to have an ending point at which all present (both improvisers and observers) understand that the improvisation being presented has come to a conclusion. Additionally, by introducing the idea of a conclusion the improvisers are once again encouraged to find a manner by which to bring their entire artistic statement to a place of resolve. This not only provides another manner by which the improviser/improvisers can find a collective cohesive artistic statement, but it also provides them a lighthouse (as it were) for which to aim.

Calling scene can occur either through mapping (i.e. once all of the improvisers arrive here or there, or once this or that happens, the improvisation has concluded), or it can occur more organically by which an individual, or several individuals, who are improvising feel as though the improvisation has run its course. As students become comfortable with calling scene during group improvisations, I will eventually allow observers to also call scene if/when they feel (based on their perspective) an improvisation has come to its logical conclusion (see Exercise #4, Chapter 12).

Try

Exercise #1: Slow Motion

This first exercise is an adaptation of the practice of Butoh (a form of Japanese dance theater), which, among several other principles, embraces the technique of slow and intentional movement. In this exercise I encourage you to experiment with time, giving your students both little time and a large amount of time to move across the floor. However, despite this being an extension of Across the Floor No Two Ways the Same, for this specific version I suggest removing the constraint that the students cannot repeat a movement.

The point of this exercise is not to expand their movement vocabulary, but to learn how to move extremely slowly and with intention. This being said, encourage your students not to simply walk or crawl, but to explore the full range of the Human Movement Buffet.

Earlier in this book I discussed that the No Two Ways the Same exercise could technically take the entire class period. At that time, I also stated that this idea was not ideal for young students who are being introduced to dance improvisation. However, understanding that this current chapter is meant for advanced improvisers, it certainly isn't out of the question to ask your students to take the entire class period to move from one side of the classroom to the other.

This being said, I again encourage you to use your years of teaching expertise. If you feel your students aren't ready for this challenge, then reduce the amount of time you are asking them to focus. However, if you feel that your students are ready, by all means please give it a try. As an added challenge, add the caveat that if a student gets to the other side of the room before the timeframe is up, they have to return back to the beginning.

One final thought, encourage your students to cross the entire space in an equitable amount of time. They should neither move too fast and then slow down, nor move too slow and the speed up to reach the end. Rather, the goal of this exercise is to learn how to move across the floor with continuous equal speed. They should consume the entire given time, while also continually exploring how to move through space in a manner that is engaging and challenging.

Exercise #2: Let them Go

This exercise is fairly straight forward. Following your chosen warmups for class, now instruct your students to begin an improvisation.

- This time, however, you will also give them the direction that they are not allowed to stop moving.
- After approximately ten minutes or so, you will notice the students moving slower and slower. This is due to the fact that continual movement without rest is exhausting.
- In spite of their apparent exhaustion, encourage them to continue.
- Remind the students of the guideline that they must keep moving at all times.

Rule #9 – Continual Movement in and of Itself Is Not Improvisation

- After you feel your students are truly exhausted, you will instruct them to find an ending.

Once the improvisation has concluded, circle the students up for conversation. Predictably one of the first statements that your students will make is, "That was exhausting." This, you will point out, was the point of the lesson. *Continual movement in and of itself is not necessarily improvisation.*

Dancers like to equate movement with improvisation, and this simplified misunderstanding can lead to improvisations that go on forever, but also go nowhere. Take this moment to discuss this idea with them, and what tools and skills they possess in order to combat this preconceived notion. Simultaneously, remind them that improvisation need not be brief either. You may notice that some, if not all, of the dance improvisations you oversee during class seem to have a specified length. This is due to the fact that many young improvisers tend to feel as though once one small arc of a dance improvisation has come and gone, this must mean the end has come. On the contrary, dance improvisations take time to build (even if mapped), and the more people you add to a dance improvisation the longer it takes to find that collective and cohesive artistic statement.

By pushing your students to go longer and longer in a dance improvisation, you teach them that while *an ending* may have been found, it doesn't have to mean that *the ending* is here. As I say to my students in class, dance improvisation can be like cooking a meal. There is much prep-work to be done, and many steps along the way. Each section has its own ending, but if I stop after merely throwing the spaghetti in the pot of water then my complete meal will never be experienced.

Exercise #3: Introducing Observers

This final exercise is actually less of an exercise and more of an idea. As mentioned, adding an audience to a dance improvisation space can be a stressful addition to a young improviser's experience. Therefore, the more ways we can repeat experiences our students have had in class, the less likely they are to regress in their learning and risk-taking.

Therefore, whenever you decide to have some of your students observe while others improvise, I recommend the following items:

- Have the observers sit in a circle around the edges of the space. While this certainly opens up the space for a larger performance space, the fact that the

Rule #9 – Continual Movement in and of Itself Is Not Improvisation

observers are seated in a circle, rather than in a line, accentuates the idea that the space is a shared space and not a performative one.
- Instruct the students who are observing to keep a note pad with them. Instruct them to take notes on items that:
  - caught their attention
  - movements they saw that piqued their interest
  - things they would like to try when they improvise
  - moments they would have loved to see more often.

By making the observation process more about the learning for the observer and less about watching a performance, the stress is taken off of the improvisers to make the improvisation feel like a performance.

As a continued aid to preventing a performative space, I also encourage you sit next to various observers while the dance improvisation is occurring, and point out areas and items of interest to you. This gives the observing students an example of how and what to look for, and it demonstrates to your students that you are engaged in what is happening.

Consider the following:

- Are the improvisers relating to one another? How are they relating? What affect does these relationships have on the observer?
- Am I able to see a cohesive artistic statement?
- Are the improvisers using some of the skills established through the various exercises in this curriculum?
- Is there a continued balance between immediate movement creation, and awareness of the environment surrounding the improvisers?
- Can I see the actual Cycle of Improvisation occurring real-time?
- Are the tools of composition being applied? If so, which ones? What affect does the implementation of this tool have on me as the observer?
- When do I feel that an idea has gone on for too long? When do I feel that an idea was dropped too soon?
- Are the improvisers able to bring back earlier movement phrases/motifs?
- Do I agree with the ending that was established? Why or why not?
- Did I recognize a mapping item? If so, what was the effect of recognizing this?

Rule #9 – Continual Movement in and of Itself Is Not Improvisation

Following the conclusion of a dance improvisation, gather both the observers and the improvisers in a circle. Ask the observers to share their thoughts, and what items they wrote down. Likewise, ask the improvisers to share their experience of being in the improvisation, and how the observers' comments help them to reflect on their experience.

Notes

Rule #10 – Be Wary of the Black Hole

Introduction

This chapter deals less with physical skills than it does with the idea that, as the saying goes, old habits die hard. Ask anyone who has tried to quit smoking, started a new workout schedule, made a New Year's resolution, or any host other commitments to stop or start a routine, and chances are you will hear about the struggles of ending an old tradition. Because we are creatures of habit, our bodies and minds dislike change. New and challenging ways of living are not built into our DNA as forms of sustainability, and therefore, unless we are vigilant in continually stretching and working the muscles (literally and figuratively) needed for continued growth, we will inevitably be pulled back into old habits by the gravitational pull of comfort, routine, and convention. This is, in some very real sense, the black hole on which this chapter is based.

Context

The black hole in dance improvisation is any and all manner in which movers fall back into ingrained habits as a result of years of training. This being said, the black hole can also be newly discovered movement motifs that, after time, settle into familiar and continual movement choices. The black hole is both an individual hazard as well as a group/collective trap. It can include

- Repeating movement phrases
- Maintaining a certain texture, quality, or level of movement
- Always mirroring others
- Being the self-proscribed "disrupter" of a dance improvisation

- Always finishing when the music ends
- Always having to map (or never mapping)
- All of the movement occurring in the center of the space
- And a host of many more items

The important item for you the instructor to be aware of is recognizing these black holes, and then assisting your students with tools to escape them. It is for this reason that I always state that improvisation instructors must, perhaps above all other dance techniques, remain actively engaged during class. As the instructor you will, like all dance technique classes, have to adapt any given day's objectives based on what occurs in class. However, unlike other technique classes, your job as a dance improvisation instructor is not to "give corrections," but rather to see, process, and then guide your students to the answer.

Therefore, the black hole applies to instructors just as much as it applies to students. An instructor can fall prey to the notion that the students have it, and therefore relax in their engagement with the students. Similarly, an instructor (remember, I include myself in all of these) can fall victim to their years of teaching and thus begin to give "corrections," rather than guidance, during a dance improvisation class. Dance improvisation is not like ballet where eventually an instructor can merely walk into the studio, give instructions and then sit back. Rather, each class should be approached as a learning opportunity for the students and the instructor.

Considerations

Black Hole #1

One black hole that may seem counterintuitive to the idea of growth and development of young dance improvisers is the notion that new is always the answer. While we do want to push our students into trying new ways of moving and being inspired, we run the risk of teaching them that "new" is right. Remember, at its core, dance improvisation is based on the idea that there is not right or wrong. Because our students want to please us, they will inherently subconsciously seek out, and therefore repeat, actions/behaviors that give them the feeling their actions are right. This is how the black hole of "new is always better" develops.

Rule #10 – Be Wary of the Black Hole

As discussed in the last chapter, context matters, especially in specific forms of dance improvisation. Couple this with today's young generation always being pulled in multiple directions via technology, and we are left with a perfect storm that lessens our students' attention spans and rewards surface-level investigation. Part of dance improvisation (especially at more mature levels) is learning how to lean into deeper investigation and exploration. Remember my cooking analogy from the previous chapter? Not only does this analogy apply to the progression of an improvisation, but it also applies to the idea that *sometimes it is best to revisit an old idea in hopes of finding something new*. Chefs do this all of the time: they retry the same recipe multiple times, changing items here and there, in hopes of finding something new and exciting. The same can be said for dance improvisation. Therefore, continue to guide and encourage your students to seek out the new, but also remind them that new for its own sake is a trap.

Black Hole #2

Another black hole worth discussing is that of touch. Now that your students have become comfortable with touching without intention, as well as touching with intention that is meant only for impulse and inspiration, you may find that one of the habits they fall into is using touch all of the time. While this is not objectionable at first, if it continues it will eventually lead to what I call the "Cuddle Puddle." This puddle is literally when all of the students are in the center of the space, moving in a fluid (I call it droopy/muddy) manner, and are simply engaging in a trance of human contact. In other words, there is pile of bodies in the middle of the room doing nothing more than squirming around.

This newfound grouping, in some regards, makes sense. In a society where physical human connection plays second fiddle to that of online affirmation, many young dancers in the America today are lacking the very basic human need of close physical contact. Hence, when our students are given the space, time, and permission to engage in this activity, they soak it up like a warm day at the beach.

The Cuddle Puddle runs two real risks when it becomes a habit:

(1) It begins to step into the realm of Contact Improvisation (something this specific book does not address in depth).
(2) It becomes a habit that, once begun, is almost impossible to escape without starting over.

Therefore, keep watch for this black hole. If/when it occurs, simply use it as a learning moment for your students. Address it through conversation, and you may be surprised what other black holes are discovered through the ensuing conversation.

Black Hole #3

The last black hole I would like to discuss is what I refer to as the "time warp." The time warp occurs when a dance improvisation has gone on for a lengthy period of time, but to the improvisers it feels like only seconds or minutes. The experience of the time warp can be intoxicating, and therefore young improvisers can start to subconsciously chase this sensation by pushing improvisations to continually last longer, all in the pursuit of this dopamine high. Just like touch, we do not want to discourage lengthy dance improvisation since many of our students will struggle with continually making their improvisations short. However, like touch, we as the instructors must remain aware at all times of the new habits that our students begin to establish and present. *Remember, habits are great until you can no longer control them; then they become additions.* Therefore, fear not the time warp, but, much like the popular song itself, it must at some point come to an end.

Try

Exercise #1: Across the Floor, but Follow Your Second Impulse

I first learned of this exercise through a friend of mine. We were teaching a dance improvisation workshop together and following my exercise of Across the Floor No Two Ways the Same, she offered this as a follow-up exercise. While I am unsure whether she came up with it on the spot, or if this was an exercise she had learned somewhere else, I find it to be a useful exercise at this point in the curriculum.

The gist of the exercise is quite simple. Have your students execute the exercise Across the Floor No Two Ways the Same (no constraints at first), but this time they must follow their second impulse every time they go to move.

Rule #10 – Be Wary of the Black Hole

- This is accomplished by allowing the students to begin moving, but then stopping immediately in order to disrupt the impulse.
- Next pause for a very brief moment (allowing a new impulse to enter the mind) and then execute that new movement impulse.
- This will occur across the entirety of the space until the student has reached the other side.
- As with the original version of this exercise, the students who are to follow will keep a close eye on the improvising students, making sure that they neither repeat a step nor follow their first impulse.

After several times performing this exercise, you may then begin to add constraints to the students as a means of increasing difficulty and movement innovation.

Exercise #2: Escaping from the Cuddle Puddle

As discussed in this chapter, the Cuddle Puddle is a very real thing. However, rather than always having to start a dance improvisation over once the Cuddle Puddle has its grip, I have found it more beneficial to give students tools in order to escape this black hole. The following two exercises are simple and easy ways to build this skill:

(1) Have your students pair up in order to revisit the Exercise #4 from
   a. Chapter 10. Depending on when the last time your students performed this exercise, you may want to revisit it in its original form.
   b. Once your students have been reacquainted with this exercise, you will now instruct them to specifically execute the exercise with the intention of ending in a Cuddle Puddle.
   c. Once the pair has reached this point they are to pause momentarily, but remain in place.
   d. The goal at this point is to now retrograde their way out of the Cuddle Puddle in the same manner, texture, and time it took them to get into it.
      This exercise can be expanded from pairs to trios, quartets, quintets, and eventually large groups.

Rule #10 – Be Wary of the Black Hole

(2) Have your students begin their dance improvisation starting in a Cuddle Puddle.
   a. Give them the goal to remove themselves from the puddle without the end result looking like a mass exodus.
   b. I recommend using this exercise only after your students have accomplished the various versions (duet, trio, quartet, etc.) of the previous exercise.
   c. Also, be sure to eventually perform this version of the exercise with observes. This way those students improvising can receive outside feedback on their solutions to escaping the Cuddle Puddle.

Exercise #3: Use Both Pop and Avant-Garde Music

Less of an exercise than a practice, I recommend using these two extremes of music as your students mature as improvisers. Using pop music is a great way to train students to listen for inspiration in music they are familiar with.

- Remember, encourage them to listen to the actual music and not just the words.
- Additionally, all pop music is written in 4/4-time signature, and therefore can become quite repetitive. It can be great practice for students to learn to be creative, in spite of music that has a monotonous time signature.
- Regarding avant-garde music, it is also great practice for students to find inspiration in music/sound that is neither "enjoyable" to listen to and that has no words or meter.

Exercise #4: Observers Call Scene

A final practice to be added to larger group improvisations is giving the observers the ability to call scene (I mentioned this in the section addressing "calling scene" in Chapter 11). Allowing this action to occur engages the observers even more while simultaneously adding a sense of spontaneity for the improvisers. The improvisers now see that they alone do not possess the power to find an ending, and that outside forces may see things differently. I also thoroughly enjoy this practice because it adds depth and richness to conversations between the observers and the improvisers following a dance improvisation.

Notes

Plus 1 – Repetition Is Comfort Food

Introduction

The subject of this chapter is as simple as its title: repetition is comforting. When considering repetition, it is important to understand this concept from both the improviser's and the observer's perspective. Both groups of individuals need and enjoy repetition for different reasons; however, the improviser is the individual who tends to struggle most with implementing this concept.

Young dance improvisers tend to think (much like young choreographers) that every time they enter a space they must create something new. On the contrary, there will never be a time where an improviser or choreographer will create anything that has never been done before in human existence. Therefore, the point of dance improvisation is to expand the improviser's movement vocabulary (giving them endless movement choices from which to draw) and not to create something completely new to human kind. *More is not always better, and new is not always the best choice.*

Context

Reaching back to our well-honed pedagogical practices, we know that repetition is the key to physical and artistic training. It is the reason our students spend so many hours in the dance studio, repeating the same steps, tasks, and exercises. Nothing (to quote a mentor of mine) "can supplement time in the studio." Therefore, the first significant key of this chapter is to understand that dance improvisation cannot be a one-and-done item. Like all dance forms, dance improvisation must be practiced, repeated, analyzed, and evaluated in order for the practitioner to grow and mature. Simply put, repetition is mandatory in order to achieve mastery.

DOI: 10.4324/9781003387084-14

Plus 1 – Repetition Is Comfort Food

Another aspect regarding repetition is the ability of the improviser to repeat movement during and throughout a dance improvisation. This can occur in two ways.

(1) The improviser repeats a singular or series of movements continuously as a means of creating duplication and/or unison.
(2) The improviser recalls and produces a movement, or series of movements, from earlier in the dance improvisation as a means of creating motif.

The latter of these two actions is perhaps the hardest to master as an improviser. After all, if one is acting upon spontaneous and rapid impulses, then how can they possibly recall any of these movements without mentally pulling themselves out of the unplanned moment?

An additional complication is that many young dancers train their time learning to remember and replicate movement produced by someone else. However, little, if any, time is dedicated to learning to spontaneously produce our own movement, let alone then be able to repeat what we just created. An obvious choice for recall/repetition could be to simply map out specific actions that a group of improvisers desire to implement throughout a dance improvisation. While this works to solve the concern regarding the need for a motif, it does little to build the mental muscle of active recall.

Therefore, my suggestion is to first rethink and redefine our definition of repetition. As movers we tend to think of repetition as only existing in shapes and action (i.e. I make a shape with my body, and then I repeat that shape). However, if we put on our choreographer's cap on for just a moment, we realize that repetition can exist in any of the five principles of choreography (Time, Space, Shape, Energy, and Form). Understanding that repetition can, and does, exist in all of these areas suddenly opens up many new worlds for us to explore. After all, returning to the same location in the dance studio (for example) is a form of repetition. Similarly, returning to a specific texture or energy of movement are also forms of repetition. Think of the endless possibilities!

While these many forms of repetition suddenly create new and exciting opportunities, they can also be overwhelming. However, some of these forms of repetition are fairly straight forward and need little, if any, continued practice. Others, however, are more elusive and difficult to repeat.

- **Space** is a simple concept to grasp, and needs little practice to master.

- The same can be said for repetition of **Energy** and **Time**; though Time can get more complicated when we explore the various modes of experiencing time versus time signatures.
- **Shape** and **Form** are the two most elusive elements to repeat, especially if the repetition is not sequential, is the repetition of. For the purposes of this chapter let us agree that Shape is simply the vast array of profiles and contours the body can make, while Form (again only for the purposes of this chapter) is simply a series of shapes strung together (i.e. a movement sequences).

The ability to recall Shape while improvising is an important skill for two reasons:

(1) It creates an automatic motif on which observers can cling should they mentally drift (i.e. get bored).
(2) It also creates smart, thinking improvisers; ones who are aware, adaptable, and intellectually in control.

These same reasons are why it is also important for improvisers to be able to repeat Form. If the goal of the first half of this book was to create free-thinking and liberated individuals, the latter half of this book is to create smart and artistically aware movers.

Considerations

Before supplying a few exercises by which your students can build these skills, I want to take brief moment to address the idea of repetition for the observer. I touched on this a bit in the previous paragraph and chapter, but a dance improvisation could (theoretically) go on forever. While none of our students will experience such a feat, eventually they will begin to create longer dance improvisations.

Individuals observing dance improvisation are no different than any other given audience. They have the same attention spans, life struggles, work schedules, and time constraints. Because of these compounding items, there is only so much mental space that any one person can give as an audience member. Therefore, if we desire to not only grow as dance improvisers, but also become ambassadors for its practice and performance, we must then take into account the needs of our audiences.

Because of its spontaneous and unstructured nature, dance improvisation can be difficult to watch for lengthy periods of time. To combat this reality, improvisers can use repetition as a means to regain an audience's attention and interest. Remember, human beings are creatures of habit, and habits are nothing more than repeated actions. Therefore, audiences subconsciously seek out repetition. If improvisers can satiate this innate human desire they not only maintain an audience's attention for the duration of a lengthy improvisation, but they also create an enjoyable experience which (ideally) leads to future attendance and audience growth.

One final note, while the below exercises provide a great beginning, be sure to explore your own ideas as they arise. Additionally, understanding that repetition is comfort food, consider how to adapt and then repeat many (if not all) of the exercises in this book as a means of making repetition recall the focus.

Try

Exercise #1: Movement Telephone

This exercise is similar to the machine game, but instead of "adding on to the machine" the goal is for the students to pass on the movement from one person to the next.

Begin the exercise by having the student stand in a line, shoulder to shoulder (think *A Chorus Line*).

- Make sure there is enough space, however, for the students to move without hitting one another.
- Choose a person at either end of the line to start the exercise. This student will make a shape (and a noise if you so desire).
- The person next to this student will then repeat the shape and sound made by the starting person and add a second shape and sound.
- The third person in the line will repeat the first and second person's shapes and sounds (in their proper order), and add a third shape and sound.
- This process continues down the line until the final student has completed all of the shapes and sounds of the entire line, and has added her/his own shape and sound.

- If at any point in the process the correct shapes and sounds are not repeated correctly, the process starts back at the beginning.
- You may also conduct this exercise with your students standing in a circle instead of a line.

A few considerations:

1. Consider starting with smaller lines so as to prevent the final student from having to remember too many shapes and sounds.
2. Once the exercise is completed, ask the final student to now serve as the beginning mover, thus sending the movement telephone back in the opposite direction.
3. After several attempts, you may either:
   a. Rearrange the line in order to prevent any singular student from being first or last.
   b. Start the exercise anywhere except with the ends of the line. In this case once the movement has reached the end of the line, it will simply be passed to the student at the other end of the line. Think of this as a round-robin option.
4. To complicate the exercise, you may do any of the following:
   a. Add more students to the line.
   b. Add a confinement to the shapes (i.e. low shapes only).
   c. Instead of shapes, expand movement choice to include sequences of movement.

Exercise #2: Group Mirror Exercise with Repetition

As a refresher, you may want to revisit Chapter 6, Exercise #3. Begin this version of the exercise with students in groups of three. As with the original version, you can expand these groups to include four or five students, but for now start with groups of three students.

- The key to this new version is that each student who becomes the leader of the group must remember the movement that she/he/they produces when they are the leader.

Plus 1 – Repetition Is Comfort Food

- Whenever the leader position is passed back to them, she/he/they must repeat (to the best of their ability) the movement they created. If done successfully each group will only produce three series of movements: one for each member of the group when they are the leader.
- The excitement in this newest version arises when a leader either passes on the leadership role before their sequence is completed, or if they chose to add on to their sequence during any future leadership moments.

After some time, you may choose to complicate this exercise by:

1. Adding more students to each group.
2. Placing confinements on what type of movement is permitted.
3. Requiring each leader to make their movement move through space.
4. Allowing students to bounce between groups.

Exercise #3: Across the Floor, but Return and Repeat

Another variation on the Across the Floor No Two Ways the Same exercise, this exercise focuses on the ability to recall one's own movement sequences. The task is simple.

- The first line of students to cross the floor (Group A) should do so without repeating steps.
- The second group of students to cross the space (Group B) are observing, ensuring that Group A's members do not repeat a step.
- However, unlike the original exercise, Group A, once having crossed the space, will go back to the beginning and try to recreate their crossing sequence.
- Group B will observe a second time, but this time trying to see if Group A's second movement sequence is close to their first movement sequence. Though you could allow the observers to use their cell phones to capture each crossing sequence (perhaps a fun exercise for younger movers), for older dancers I recommend watching solely. This not only keeps each group engaged, but it also builds movement recall in the observer as well as the mover.

- Once Group A has completed their second sequence, Group B may now begin.
- The exercise continues until all groups have successfully crossed the space twice.
- Once all groups have successfully crossed the space, repeat the exercise but travel in the opposite direction.

At any point in time you may desire to add a constraint.

As always, I suggest starting slowly and simply before building complexity. Consider starting first with hopping and changing shapes, adding the ability to recall all shapes on the second pass. Following completion of this, add constraints to this particular version of the exercise (i.e. shapes only) before moving onto movement phrases that travel.

As a reminder on how to complicate the original version of this exercise, revisit Exercise #1, Chapter 5.

Exercise #4: Repeating Clap Exercise

The execution of this newest version is the same as the original.

- Students sitting around the circle will make a singular/sound and the person in the middle of the circle will use each sound as inspiration for their movement choice.
- The seated students will need to remember the pitch/tone/texture of sound they make, and do their best to replicate it every time they provide auditory stimuli to the person in the center.
- The seated students need not speak/make noise in any given pattern (all the better if they do not), but they do need to ensure that each time they make their noise it is the same as before.

The purpose for this newly introduced constraint is that each time the person in the middle of the circle hears a specific sound, she/he must recreate the same shape/movement as the first time they heard it.

This practice allows the students in the center to work on both movement memory recall, while also continually working on using external stimuli as a source for inspiration. Remember, start slowly and then build in difficulty. This exercise should be fun and engaging.

After several rounds of this exercise, you may decide to add difficulty by:

1. Increasing the number of students seated in the circle.
2. Allowing the seated students to increase the tempo by which they make their noises.
3. Allow the seated students to make two noises each. This will increase the difficulty, as the student in the center will now have twice as many sounds and shapes to remember. It will also require the seated students to remember two noises now, rather than one.
4. Instruct the student in the center of the circle to create small movement phrases for each sound, rather than a simple shape.
5. Add a second person to the middle of the circle. One person reacts to the sounds, and the second person must mimic the first person.

Notes

14 Additional Considerations and Concluding Thoughts

Introduction

Thus far, this book has focused on dance improvisation within the context of contemporary and modern dance. However, many of the principles, exercises, and practices are completely transferable to other forms of dance. For example, many of the exercises in this book could simply have the added constraint of ballet vocabulary added as a means of challenging our ballet students. Similarly, the idea of creating movement based on a toned, metered sound scape is an inherent principle of jazz dance.

Needless to say, this book, though written from a contemporary dance lens, is sure to benefit your students in their various dance studies. In fact, I encourage you to consider adding this book as a tool for improvisation in all of the dance styles your studio offers. Feel free to play with the ideas and exercises in order to make them better accommodate each dance genre. Ultimately, you could create an entirely new improvisation curriculum for each dance genre by using this book as your foundation. Not only will this help differentiate your studio/program, but it will also assist your students in understanding that all things are connected, especially as it relates to dance improvisation.

Context

Another item worth mentioning is that you need not offer dance improvisation as its own separate class. Time is limited (both for students and teachers), and adding one more class might be too much for your business/program. If this is the case, then I encourage you to consider how you might add improvisation into each of your classes. Whether you sprinkle it throughout a class, or add it to the beginning or ending of a class, adding dance improvisation into each of

DOI: 10.4324/9781003387084-15

Additional Considerations and Concluding Thoughts

your dance classes is a great way to assist your students with dipping their toes into this new experience. Additionally, by integrating dance improvisation into your already existing classes, you assist your students in seeing the direct correlation between what is learned in improvisation and what is learned in their other dance classes.

It is also worth mentioning at this point the various other forms of dance improvisation. As discussed earlier in this book, improvisation is not new to many dance forms. Tap dance, Vernacular Jazz Dance, and Hip Hop all have improvisation built within their training and pedagogy. Similarly, Contact Improvisation has been a codified dance practice in the United States since the 1970s, and improvisation (both within a given dance context and as a codified dance vocabulary) has existed since the earliest days of humankind. Many traditional social dances from across the globe include improvisation as a part of both training and performance. Everything from traditional West African, to Flamenco, to Capoeira, to the Western Square Dance infuse improvisation as a method of practice and mastery.

With limited space in this book, it is important to acknowledge some of these codified dance techniques and their usage of dance improvisation. If for no other reason, it is important that we recognize these longstanding and respected dance practices for their histories and contributions to the advancement of dance and dance improvisation. Additionally, there is much to learn from these dance forms as they relate to dance improvisation. Beginning, or continuing, our training in these other dance forms only adds to our growth as teachers, artists, and humans.

For anyone unfamiliar with the term Vernacular Jazz Dance, it is helpful to start with a basic definition. The word vernacular simply means "of the people." Whether we are speaking about speech, movement, art, music, fashion, or any other form of communication and expression, the term vernacular simply refers to items such as these being born/created by collective individuals or groups. Therefore, Vernacular Jazz Dance would be a genre of jazz dance that was born/created by the everyday person.

There are several books written on the history of jazz dance in America, and I would highly recommend reading many of them if you are new to Vernacular Jazz Dance[1] Since Vernacular Jazz Dance was born out of the social aspects of its surrounding culture (including items such as oral tradition, call and response, community, and deep integration between sound and movement), improvisation became an inherent part of Vernacular Jazz Dance. Two examples of this are the Charleston and the Lindy Hop. Both of these dance steps were birthed

Additional Considerations and Concluding Thoughts

out of a long tradition of social dances, created as a commentary for a specified moment in time, and eventually gave way to other social dance steps.

For the purposes of dance improvisation, these two Vernacular Jazz Dance steps (Charleston and Lindy Hop) have a basic version that was created in order for them to be shared, but ultimately personal flair and creativity (i.e. improvisation) were meant to be added. Camille A. Brown has a wonderful video online discussing this subject. I would highly suggest that you and your students participate in workshops, conventions, and master classes where Vernacular Jazz Dance is taught. Not only will it open new doors to moving and musicality, but it will also benefit the study of contemporary dance improvisation since Vernacular Jazz Dance focuses on improvisation within its own set style/vocabulary.

One cannot speak of Vernacular Jazz Dance without also speaking about Tap dance. Both share the same long history, and many of the aspects of Vernacular Jazz Dance are also inherent in Tap dance. However, Tap dance holds one unique skill set that separates it from many of the other concert dance forms in the United States: the body is both the music and movement maker.

Tap dance holds the special distinction of being one of the few dance forms (including Flamenco, Stomping, and several others) where the body simultaneously produces the music and sounds, as well as the movement. This added complexity makes the ability to improvise within Tap dance that much more complex, and that much more genius. Tap dancers must not only take into account their own desired movement improvisation, but they must also take into account how their musical improvisation will affect the other musicians (be it other Tap dancers or jazz instrumentalists) with whom they are engaging. Because of this, improvisation within Tap dance tends to follow that of other jazz musicians: musical improvisation can be an expression of personal flair and creativity, but ultimately the improvisation is subject to the time signature, swing, key signature, and overall coherency of the music and ensemble.

If your students haven't already done so, I highly recommend that they attend a Tap dance concert. Specifically, I recommend that they attend a Tap dance company who uses only live musicians, who focuses on rhythm and hoofing styles, and whose performers regularly improvise within the dance pieces presented. Additionally, I recommend that any dance student begin studying Tap dance (if even at a basic level), as a means of adding to their musicality, timing, rhythm, and dance improvisational arsenal.

Continuing in the lineage of Vernacular Jazz Dance and Tap dance, I would be remiss to discuss improvisation in dance without also discussing Hip Hop.

Let me first reiterate what my colleague and friend Professor Crystal Frazier[2] always reiterates when discussing Hip Hop: "Hip Hop is a culture, not just music or dance steps." More to the point, Hip Hop has five original elements (as established by Afrika Bambaataa), only one of which is actually tied to dance (i.e. Breaking).

This being said, improvisation (known actually as freestyling) has always held a place in the various dance forms found within Hip Hop. Specifically, in a Breaking cipher, dancers battle one another by laying down both similar steps to which their rival Breaker performed, but also executing their own personal variation and style within the given context of the battle. This form of call and response can be traced back to the earliest days of dance competitions in the United States (such as the famous buck-and-wing competition between Bill Robinson and Harry Swinton), and even earlier dance forms from various cultures and peoples across the globe, but ultimately many dance forms within Hip Hop dance have integrated freestyling (dance improvisation) as an integral part of self-expression and training.

While I highly recommend that your dancers train in any form of traditional Hip Hop, I specifically recommend the form of House. House dance (of all of the styles of Hip Hop) encourages personal improvisation and freedom, without the need for the death-defying skills of Breaking. Regardless, any historic/traditional Hip Hop training will only further expand a dancer's improvisation skillset, musicality, cultural awareness, and polyrhythmic and isolatory movement skills.

A final version of dance improvisation I feel the need to address is Contact Improvisation. While some of the basics of Contact Improvisation were discussed and explored in this book (i.e. touch as stimuli for creativity), the practice and mastery of Contact Improvisation is a life-long commitment. Contact Improvisation, sometimes called "non-traditional partnering," is so much more than mere physical contact and lifting. It is a complex theory and practice that relies heavily on training, trust, and shared weight. Founded in the 1970s in the United States by Steve Paxton, this specific form of dance improvisation will surely expand your students' physical and artistic skills. Not only will they learn new and exciting lifts and partnering exercises, but they will delve even deeper into some of the ideas presented in this book. The great news is that the training provided by this book gives all dancers a solid foundation by which they can begin their journey into Contact Improvisation.

There are, of course, many more forms of improvisation in dance throughout the world, in addition to the ones mentioned in this chapter. All dance forms offer unique and specific skills in improvisation meant to enhance training, execution and performance of each dance form. In the ideal world we would study all of these wonderful dance forms as a means of both continuing our training as dance improvisers, as well as an act of cultural sharing and collaboration. This being said, find the dance styles that make the most sense for you and your students, and remember that all forms of dance improvisation can, and should, inform all others. Just as training in jazz dance increases one's musicality for ballet class, training in multiple styles of dance improvisation inherently informs and grows all other areas of improvisation.

In addition to the many forms of improvisation in dance through the world, there are an equal number of ways in which improvisation is incorporated in the other forms of art. I already quoted Wynton Marsalis earlier in this book and his thoughts on improvising as a jazz musician. Similar to jazz dance, jazz music has a long and rich history of improvisation as a part of its training and performance. So too does theater.

While many theatrical shows aim to produce consistent productions for their audiences, actors, and directors know, and even embrace, real-time adaptation as a part of their performative experience (i.e. a slight pause for the audience laughter to subside, or a slight change in tempo to accommodate that evening's rhythm of a scene). As seen by the earliest exercises in this book, improvisation is an innate part of an actor's training.

Visual artists are, by their very nature, improvisers. Whether creating a new painting, sculpture, or installation, the creation process is a perfect reflection of the Cycle of Improvisation. And I cannot mention improvisation in art without mentioning the masters of improvisation: DJs. These individuals perform improvisation every time they play a venue; mixing and matching music and lights in real-time in order to engage the audience in an evening-long experience of emotional highs and passionate ecstasy.

Considerations

Improvisation is everywhere and is in all things. This being said, because of its omnipresent nature it can easily be misconstrued as something that simply happens. If you have gained nothing more from this workbook, I hope that you have gained an appreciation for the complexity and training necessary in order to become a proficient and masterful improviser.

Additional Considerations and Concluding Thoughts

I would like to stress one last time that this book is not the end of the journey for you and your students. Rather, it is merely the beginning. As discussed, increasing one's proficiency in dance improvisation has inherent benefits to all other codified dance forms. You will find, in time, that your students' musicality is more mature, their creativity is larger, their attention to detail is more refined, their performance quality is further developed, their communication is clearer, and their happiness (yes, I said it – their happiness) is fuller. It may sound like the world is being promised, and in some regard it is, but ultimately the first step begins with you. As I said early in the book, you have the years of pedagogical training, now simply follow the steps of this yellow-brick road and see where it takes you.

Try

I leave you with one final thought. Every time I teach an introductory dance improvisation class, I discuss with the students what to expect. Parallel to the contract I made with you at the beginning of this book, I similarly promise my students that I will do my best to undo all of the preconceived worries and fears they possess regarding dance improvisation. I always conclude my conversation with these students, and now this book, with the following statement:

> I cannot promise you that dance improvisation will change **the** world, but I can promise you that dance improvisation will change **your** world; and the old world as you knew and experienced it will cease to exist. Welcome to a new world. - MF

Citations

1. Personally I recommend reading *Jazz Dance: A History of the Roots and Branches* by Lindsay Guarino and Wendy Oliver. Gainesville: University Press of Florida, 2015; *Rooted Jazz Dance: Africanist Aesthetics and Equity in the Twenty-First Century* by Lindsay Guarino, Carlos R.A. Jones, and Wendy Oliver. Gainesville: University Press of Florida, 2022.
2. Frazier, Crystal. Professor, Pointe Park University. 2019-Present.

Notes

15 Sample Class Curriculums

Introduction

The following are a few sample classes structures based on the scaffolding of my **10 Rules of Improvisation: Plus 1** discussed in Chapter 2. While these examples are by no means exhaustive, nor do they guide you through an entire year's planning, they are meant to guide you toward developing dance improvisation classes that meet the needs of your students, the time constraints of your classes, and the annual curriculum of your studio/classroom. As I stated in Chapter 1, you alone know the needs of your students, studio, and community best. Therefore, adapt the proposed exercises, teachings, and instructions of this book as best suits your situation and circumstances.

Context

Most dance improvisation classes I teach at the university level either meet 50 minutes per class period, three days per week, or they meet 90 minutes per class period, two days per week. For simplicity's sake, the class samples provided in this chapter are written with a 50-minute class period (meeting three days per week) in mind. Feel free to adapt the times allotted for each exercise to fit your class schedule/s. Also feel free to sprinkle the exercises provided in this book throughout your already existing dance courses. Just remember that exercises later in the book are reserved only for more advanced improvisers. Therefore, if you do not have a dedicated dance improvisation course, then it will take much longer to work through the entire curriculum and eventually implement exercises in the later chapters.

DOI: 10.4324/9781003387084-16

Considerations

Before diving into specific class structures and examples, I feel it important to first address how I might implement the entire 10 Rules of Improvisation: Plus 1 curriculum throughout a 15-week semester. This layout addresses (1) how I may plan out when certain rules will be introduced, and (2) how long I anticipate my students to grasp them. However, change and adaptation are always a part of the curricular equation, and therefore, I use this layout as a guideline rather than an unchangeable rule.

As an added sidenote, I have supplied many more exercises in this book than I could accomplish in a single semester. Hopefully, this abundance of material allows you to adapt your implementation of this curriculum, while also giving you multiple ways to address any particular skill/idea. Remember, this layout is based on a dance improvisation class that meets 50 minutes per class period, three days per week.

Finally, for more curriculum examples, video demonstrations of exercises in this book, and additional resources for both Dance Improvisation and Choreography, visit my webpage www.mfarmerdance.com

Proposed Semester Layout

- Week 1
    - Rule #1 – Introduced
- Week 2
    - Rule #1 – Continued
    - Rule #2 – Introduced
- Week 3
    - Rule #1 and Rule #2 – Continued
- Week 4
    - Rule #1 and Rule #2 – Continued
    - Rule #3 – Introduced
- Week 5
    - Rule #3 – Continued
    - Rule #4 – Introduced

Sample Class Curriculums

- Week 6
  - Rule #3 and Rule #4 – Continued
- Week 7
  - Rule #5 – Introduced
- Week 8
  - Rule #5 – Continued
  - Rule #6 – Introduced
- Week 9
  - Rule #5 and Rule # 6 – Continued
  - Rule #7 – Introduced
- Week 10
  - Rule # 7 – Continued
  - Rule #8 – Introduced
- Week 11
  - Rule #8 – Continued
  - Rule #9 – Introduced
- Week 12
  - Rule #9 – Continued
  - Rule #10 – Introduced
- Week 13
  - Rule #9 and Rule #10 – Continued
  - Rule #11 – Introduced
- Week 14
  - Rule #11 – Continued
- Week 15
  - Fully implemented improvisation sessions, followed by analysis

Try

Below are a few class structure examples based on the semester layout in this chapter. Again, I have supplied more exercises per chapter than I could

Sample Class Curriculums

implement in a given semester. Therefore, feel free to change out exercises supplied below with alternative exercises from the corresponding chapter.

- **Week 1**
    - Classes 1–3: What is Dance Improvisation and Rule #1 Introduced

    Warm-ups
        - Juggling Exercise (Chapter 2) – ten minutes
        - Walking Exercise #1 (Chapter 2) – five minutes
        - Walking Exercise #2 (Chapter 2) – five minutes

    Traveling Through Space
        - Wiggling Exercise (Chapter 3) – ten minutes
        - Run, Stop, Change/Change…Run, Stop, Clap with Change/Change Same (Chapter 3) – ten minutes
            - *Across the Floor No Two Ways the Same (Chapter 3) – Introduce this in Class 3

    Center Work
        - Return to Walking Exercise #2 (Chapter 2) – ten minutes
            - Machine Game (Chapter 4) – *Introduce this in Class 3 in preparation for the next weeks lesson.

- **Week 2**
    - Classes 1–3: Rule #1 Continued, and Introduce Rule #2

    Warm-ups
        - Juggling Exercise (Chapter 2) – ten minutes
        - Walking Exercise #2 (Chapter 2) – five minutes

    Traveling Through Space
        - Wiggling Exercise (Chapter 3) – five minutes
        - Run, Stop, Change/Change…Run, Stop, Clap with Change/Change Same (Chapter 3) – five minutes
        - Across the Floor No Two Ways the Same (Chapter 3) – ten minutes

    Center Work
        - Machine Game (Chapter 4) – five minutes
        - The Object Game (Chapter 4) – ten minutes

Sample Class Curriculums

- **Week 6**
  - Classes 1–3: Rule #3 and Rule #4 Continued

  Warm-ups
    - Tapping into Your Proprioception (Chapter 6) – ten minutes
    - Traveling Through Space
    - Revisiting Across the Floor No Two Ways the Same (Chapter 5) – ten minutes
    - Center Work
    - Revisit the Clapping Game (Chapter 5) – ten minutes
    - Mirroring Exercise (Chapter 5) – ten minutes
    - Negative Space Exploration (Chapter 6) – ten minutes

- **Week 10**
  - Classes 1–3: Rule #7 Continued, and Rule #8 Introduced

  Warm-ups
    - Entry Point #2 (Chapter 9) – ten minutes
    - Clapping Exercise but with Sound (Chapter 10) – ten minutes
    - Traveling Through Space
    - Entry Point #1 (Chapter 9) – ten minutes
    - Center Work
    - Moving Away or To the Touch Expanded (Chapter 10) – ten minutes
    - Group Mirror Exercise (Chapter 9) – ten minutes

- **Week 14**
  - Classes 1–3: Rule #11 Continued, and continued focus on entire curriculum

  Warm-ups
    - Slow Motion (Chapter 11) – five minutes
    - Traveling Through Space
    - Across the Floor, but Return and Repeat (Chapter 13) – ten minutes
    - Center Work
    - Escaping from the Cuddle Puddle (Chapter 12) – five minutes
    - Repeating Clap Exercise (Chapter 13) – ten minutes

Sample Class Curriculums

<u>Improvisations</u>
- Group Improvisations – anyone can call scene (20 minutes)

- **Week 15**

At this point, your students should be able to enter group improvisations with confidence. I due recommend that you still begin the class with a small warmup as a means of centering their minds and bodies in the space.

Notes

Author, Matthew Farmer

Index

Note: *Italic* page numbers refer to figures.

acceleration 149
accumulation 148
adaptation/adaptability 72, 74, 80, 101, 106, 120–121, 136, 140, 147, 150, 176, 180
animal movement 31–32; *see also* movement
arc, self-awareness of 19–20
artistic: expression 146–147; impulses 47; skills 175; training 59
artistry 14–15, 38, 101
assorted auditory sounds 130
audience 145–146, 149–150, 152, 165–166, 176
autonomy 49, 73
avant-garde music 161

ballet 23, 36, 61–62, 64–65, 144, 157, 172, 176; class 36; solo 144–145
bear crawling 31–32
bias 29; creative 128; intrinsic 86; movement 145; physical 102
binary/non-binary thinking 36, 38, 50, 73
biological impulses 50–53
black hole in dance improvisation: considerations 157–159; context 156–157; description of 156; exercise 159–161; recognizing 157
bodies, senses of 132
body parts 33, 40, 64, 86, 94–98, 106, 108, 139
Butoh, practice of 150–151

calling scene 149–150, 161
cannon 148
caring 84, 100, 143
"Change-Change" instruction 42
change partners 68, 90, 104, 110
chaos 21, 130, 149
children, aptitude of 48–49
choice-making 101
choreographers/choreography 1–2, 101, 113–115, 163; generation 8–9; learning and regurgitating 9; principles of 164; work 114
Clap-Clap 42
clapping game 67
class 37–38, 85–86; actual improvisation portion of 63; discussion 22; engagement, guidelines for 22; etiquette, principles for 22; practice outside of 73; structure 17, 25, 61–62, 72, 180–182

Index

classroom 2, 4, 13, 22–25, 49, 101, 105, 141, 151
cognitive dissonance 24
collaboration 176
color 62, 65, 133, 138, 140, 147
communal: experience 84–85; improvisation 100; setting 84, 87
communication 173; community and 101; physical 69; skills 86; verbal 69
community 100, 102; and communication 101; idea of 100; improvisational 102; students understanding of 101; understanding and experience of 101
complexity 12, 79, 90, 169, 174, 176
compositional tools 148–149
compromise 74, 80, 101
conformity 37, 49
constraints 64, 66; in exercise 67; types of 65
contact improvisation 106, 125, 134–135, 173, 175; basics of 175; practice and mastery of 175
contemporary dance 13, 172, 174
continual movement 143–144; calling scene 149–150; collective and cohesive artistic expression 146–147; compositional tools 148–149; context 144; dance improvisation with performance 144–146; exercise 150–154; mapping 147
continual practice 20
continual vocal guidance 93
continuation 91, 101
conversation 8, 12, 25–26, 30, 95–96, 101, 112–114, 127, 129, 135, 141, 152, 159, 177
counterpoint 148
crawling 48; bear 31–32; crab 31–32; lizard 32; monkey 31–32

creative/creativity 14–15, 23, 36–38, 49, 59, 75, 86, 174; biases 128; exploration 37; movement generation 43; opportunity for 94
Cuddle Puddle 158, 160–161
cultural/culture 29, 35, 47; baggage 93, 129, 145; biases 18; norms 30, 36; sharing 176
curricular: approach 19; pyramid 20–21, *21*
curriculum 6, 13, 18–20, 23, 30, 43, 60, 71, 84, 93, 112, 125, 127, 143; for dance genre 172; dance improvisation 17, 25; implementation of 180; levels of 20; portions of 62–63; progression-based 2; progressive 2

dance 17; classes 25; competitions 175; contemporary 172; forms 22, 39, 163, 176; modern 172; movement vocabulary 7; studios 9, 11, 17, 23–25, 29–30, 73, 85–86, 163–164; styles 172; techniques 2, 8–9, 11, 23, 36–37, 62, 173; training 6
dance improvisation 6, 39, 43, 55, 63, 85, 102, 112–115, 119, 152, 159, 172, 176; application in 102; assessment 9; beauty of approaching 61; benefits of 13–14; challenges 24; concept 9; contributions 114; conversations surrounding 113; course 179; curriculum 25, 60; cycle of 11–12, *12*; description of 1; education and practice of 20; elements of 61–62; flow of 19; forms of 10, 113, 158, 173; group 117; idea of 6, 61–62; individuals observing 165; integrating 173; learning 84; manner and approach to 127; memories of 116; methods of 12; movements 113–114, 164;

pedagogical approach to teaching 1–2; performance 114–116, 146–147; power of 20; practicing 8, 116; practitioners of 14; primary and prevailing principle on 11; proficiency in 176; purposes of 112, 114, 144, 174; semester layout 180–184; teaching and experiencing 2; techniques struggle with 10; time spent in 18; usage of 173; workshop 159

dancers 2, 10, 127, 133

dance training 8, 59; forms of 37; integral part of 71; performance-focused 37–38, 49, 59

debriefings 81, 90, 96

decelerate/ritardando 149

dualistic/non-dualistic thinking 36

education 47; of dance improvisation 20; system 36

embarrassment 24, 36

empathetic reaction 101

energy/dynamic 49, 131, 165

engagement: class 22; mental 93; with students 157; students understanding of 101

environment/environmental: change 28; experience movement in 76

epiphanies 120–123

exercise 3, 13, 17, 25–27, 30, 33, 42, 44, 51–52, 60–64, 69, 71–74, 77, 79, 81, 88, 92, 95–96, 102, 118–119, 122, 165; across the floor, but return and repeat 168–169; Across the Floor Exercise No Two Ways the Same Exercise 102–105, 108–110; adapt/expand on 92, 138, 140; alternative 181–182; and approaches 112; "back to the beginning" for 27, 45, 67, 109, 117, 151, 168; clap exercise 169–170; clapping 55–57, 137–138; classes of performing 44; from class to class 42; continuation of mirroring 77–78; Cuddle Puddle 160–161; duration of 93; form of 43; goal of 98; group mirror exercise with repetition 167–169; group mirroring 78, *78*; by instructing dancers 41; introducing observers 152–154; iteration of 121–122; let them go 151–152; listening to music, picking an indicator, explore the indicator 135–137; machine game 52–54; movement telephone 166–167; moving away or to the touch–expanded 139–140; moving toward and away from touch 105–108; object game 54–55; original version of 92; progressive levels for 96–97; purpose of 69, 75–76; resulting effect of 40; return to object game 138–139; simplicity of 41; slow motion 150–151; sound indicator and repeat 136; spy 140–141; strength-building 30–31; transitioning version of 74; use both pop and avant-garde music 161; variations of 136; version of 92, 137; video demonstrations of 180

exploration 33, 49; creative/creativity 37; free-based 2; movement 39, 84–85, 144, 146; negative space 80–81; physical source for 86

expression 146–147, 173

external non-biological impulses 50–53

external stimuli/stimulus 51, 102

faith practices 36, 84

familiarity 117

flexibility 49

Frazier, Crystal 175

free-based exploration 2

freedom 7, 18, 24–25, 37, 49, 87, 138, 140

Index

games 1, 17, 51–52, 61–62
generational baggage 129
giggles 67–68
globe via social media 22–23
grand allegro 61
group dance improvisations 100, 112, 117; *see also* dance improvisations
group improvisation 18–19, 116–118, 122, 143; *see also* dance improvisations
group mirroring exercise 77–80, *78*, 120–123
Guideline for Class Engagement 23

habits 29, 84, 127
hearing 131–132
hierarchy of importance 73
high-level movement 64
Hip Hop 37–39, 173, 175
historical baggage 129, 145
hugging 88
Human Movement Buffet 9, 60, 63, 68, 102, 113, 151

Iannacone, Steven 40, 43
Ido Portal 48
imaginations 2, 37, 49, 55, 86, 88, 132
immediacy 14–15
immediate gratification 25
improvisation 124; complicated and multifaceted approaches to 73–74; cycle of 101, 117, 176; equate movement with 152; forms of 175–176; history of 176; idea of 71; path and safety rails for 147; practicing 145; rules of 47, 116; study and practice of 14
improviser 128, 141, 144, 147, 154, 157, 159, 163–165; degree of expectation of 146; experience 152; movement vocabulary 163; sense of spontaneity for 161

impulses/stimuli 85, 120, 134; artistic 47; biological 50; category chart 50, *51*; contact and control of 50; external 132; for movement generation 88; in music 131–132; negative connotation toward 50; non-biological 50–51; personal 47, 74; source of 128; tactile 134–135; types of 51; visual 133–134
incitement 50
inclination 50, 86, 106
independence 36–37
individual/individuals: creative practice 6; creativity 37; improvisation 143
inspiration 50–51, 84–85, 127–128, 134, 170; external 132; in music 131–132; opportunity for 94; source of 128
instructors 3, 9, 96, 157, 159
intentional mindfulness 92
interactions 36, 88, 125
internal non-biological impulses 50–51, 53
intrinsic bias 86
irrationality 50

jazz dance 7, 39, 59, 61, 144; genre of 173; history of 173; training in 176
juggling 26–28, 61–62, 72; actions and timing needed for 26; exercise 29, 72; objects 26; students' progress in 72

lateral thinking 37, 106
laughter 11, 22–24, 67–68, 176
leadership 78–79, 89, 168
learning 84–85, 127
levels 149
live musicians 174
lizard crawling 32
locations/environments 87
low-level movement 64

machine game 54–55, 61–62, 88, 90, 166
mapping 147, 150

Index

Marsalis, Wynton 7, 176
medium-level movement 64
melodies 129
mental: engagement 93; fatigue 81; health 48; strength 32
meterless soundscape 130–131
mindfulness, intentional 92
mirror/mirroring exercise 67–69, 118–120
mobility 48–49
modern dance 172
monkey crawling 31–32
movement 17, 133–134, 138, 140; biases 74, 145; choices 156; continual and rapid 68; creation/creativity 127, 144; exploration 39, 144, 146; generation 84, 88, 113–114, 134; habits 127; improvisation 174; motifs 156; sequences 168; styles 113; telephone 166–167; vocabulary 8, 59, 64, 66–67, 102, 113, 132
multiple stimuli 119–120
music/musical 127–128, 131, 135; accompaniment 128; avant-garde 161; Beethoven 129; Carnatic 129; category chart 129, *129*; digital versions of 128; genre of 129; idea of 128–129; improvisation 174; impulses and inspiration in 131–132; pop 161; subcategories 129; theory 131

negative space 123; exercise 123–124; exploration 80–81
Negative Space Explorer 81
Newton's Third Law 11–12
noises 52–53, 74, 129, 170
non-biological impulses 50–52, 54; external 50–53, 85–86, 128, 132; internal 50–51, 53, 127
non-traditional partnering 175
norms 30
nuance 101

object game 61–62
observers 145–146, 153–154
order 149
originality 37

painting 176
partner/partnering 95–96; exercises 175; mirror exercise 121; non-traditional 175; skills 93
passive observer 25
patience 60
Paxton, Steve 175
pedagogical practices 25, 163
performance 173; art form 19; focused dance training 37–38, 49; practice of 61; quality 14–15, 176; space 153
personal: biases 84; choice/voice 38; creativity 37–38; expression 145; impulses 47, 74; movement biases 19; movement generation 113; space 112
petite allegro 61
philosophical conversations 35
physical: ability 49; actions 147; biases 102; communication 69; contact 18–19, 87, 91, 101, 158; environment 87; execution 38; harm 39; health 48; improvisation 13; impulses 48; injury 81; response/reaction 135; skills 156, 175; stimuli 86; strength 32; touch 93; training 59; trauma 93
play equipment 47–48
playfulness 172
pop music 161
position 2, 41, 79, 81–82, 93–99, 117, 133, 148, 153, 168
practice 20, 101
private/safe space 93
professional/progressions 13, 96–97; curriculum 2; decorum 49; pyramid, level of 19; theories 3; training program 12–13

193

Index

proprioception 74–76, 91
prowess 1, 9, 13–14, 38, 40

rap 129
reality 59–60, 87, 146, 166
reinterpretation 55
repetition 67, 149, 163, 166; definition of 164; exercise 166–169; forms of 164; group mirror exercise with 167–168
resting positions 97–98
retrograde 149, 160
rightness 36–37
right vs. wrong concept 35–36
risk-taking 14–15, 141, 152
Robinson, Ken 37
Rohr, Richard 36

Samba dance 129
sample class curriculums 179; considerations 180; context 179; proposed semester layout 180–181
school 4, 11, 21–22, 25–26, 37, 47, 74, 100
sculpture 176
segmentation 36
self-awareness, sense of 115
self-discovery 71–72
self-improvisation 84
self-indulgent 100
sense of self 87
shape 132–133, 138, 140, 165
sight 132
simplicity 12
sink/swim method 116
size/scale 133–134, 138, 140
skepticism 24
skills 11, 37, 76, 80, 113–114, 145, 160, 165, 180; artistic 175; of Breaking 175; building 101; communication 86; developing 74; in improvisation 175–176; partner/partnering 93; physical 156, 175
smell 132
social/societal: attention/embarrassment 36; baggage 145; media 22–23, 100; norms 30, 36
society 29, 35, 47, 49
solo improvisation 122
somatic mannerisms 102
sounds 129, 131, 135; assorted auditory 130; indicators 136–137; principles of 132; toned/tone 130; toneless 130
soundscapes 10, 129–130, 136; meterless 130–131
space 135–136, 153, 164; additional bodies in 101; for conversations 114; performative 153; personal 112
spontaneity 38–39, 161
spur conversation 104, 136
stamina 47
STEAM (Science, Technology, Engineering, Arts, and Math) 37
STEM (Science, Technology, Engineering, and Math) 37
stillness 148–149
strength 47; building exercise 30–31; mental 32; physical 32
structure 17–18, 25, 61–62, 72, 130–131, 180–181
students 9, 19, 22–24, 27–28, 33, 38–39, 41, 65, 69, 74, 76–77, 89, 96, 116, 135; ability 39; action and noise 52–53; active conversation with 93; behavior 22–23; creativity and movement vocabulary 59; daily warmup 72; desire of 143; engagement with 157; external impulses 54; to idea of touch 93; ideas of right vs. wrong 35; imaginations 55; in learning 39; physical, mental, and emotional safety

of 39; physical and artistic skills 175; physical tasks 31; proprioception 75–76; return to conversation circle 30; switched roles 75; training 38, 49
studio/classroom 29, 179
style/technique 61
subtraction/dispersion 148
suspension/fermata 149
sustainability 156
symbiotic relationship 47
symmetry 149

Tactile Encyclopedia 95
tactile stimuli 134–135, 140
tap dance 38–39, 144, 173–174; complexity 174; lineage of 174–175; rhythms in 143; studying 174
taste 132, 144
teaching/teachers 2–3, 10, 23, 35, 39, 58–59, 63, 65–66, 101, 173; dance improvisation 25–26; expertise 151; process of 91
technology 48, 101, 158
temperature 134, 140
10 Rules of Improvisation: Plus 1 1–3, 12–13, 51, 117, 179–180
texture 65, 131, 133–134, 138, 140
theory/vocabulary 6, 10, 13
thinking-creative movement artists 128
time 65–66, 131, 143, 165–166; constraints 165; investment 25; warp 159
toned/tone: sounds 130; structured phrases 130
toneless: sounds 130; structured phrases 130
Touch History 85

touch/touching 87–88, 96–97, 132, 134, 158; exercise 124–125; physical 93
traditional/traditionalism 49; dance, feel and structure of 17–18; movement choices 114
training 8, 13, 37, 51–52, 101, 145, 173; artistic 59; complexity and 176; in jazz dance 176; physical 59; program, progression-based 12–13; students 38, 49
transitions 31–33, 117
trust 23, 56, 60–61, 75, 89, 95, 106, 175

unison 114, 123–124, 148, 164
United States, dance: classes in 127–128; competitions in 175; forms in 174; in training in 128
unpredictability 14, 101

verbal communication 69
vernacular jazz dance 173–175
vertical dynamics 53, 91
visual: artists 176; indicator 138; inspiration 141; stimuli 133–134, 138, 140–141
Vitruvian Man 80–81, 106–108, 139
vocabulary 6–8, 10, 13, 59, 113–115, 134, 145, 163, 173–174
vocal instructions 41–42
vulnerability 55–56

walking exercises 28–33, 73, 117–118
warm-up 28–29, 61, 71, 151; daily 72; stationary 62; steps and progressions of 27–28
wiggling 39–40
wrongness 21, 36–37

For Product Safety Concerns and Information please contact our EU
representative GPSR@taylorandfrancis.com
Taylor & Francis Verlag GmbH, Kaufingerstraße 24, 80331 München, Germany

www.ingramcontent.com/pod-product-compliance
Lightning Source LLC
Chambersburg PA
CBHW050536300426
44113CB00012B/2126